Sean O'Casey

THE IRISH WRITERS SERIES

James F. Carens, General Editor

SEAN O'CASEY

Bernard Benstock

Lewisburg
BUCKNELL UNIVERSITY PRESS

Associated University Presses, Inc.
Cranbury, New Jersey 08512

Second Printing, June, 1972

822
015B
1970

ISBN: 0-8387-7748-1 (cloth)
        0-8387-7618-3 (paper)
Printed in the United States of America

Contents

Sean O'Casey: Chronology

1880 Born 30 March; last child of Susan and Michael Casey. Name: John Casey. Date of birth often listed erroneously as 1884.

1886 Death of Michael Casey; the family begins the serious decline into poverty.

1894 At work as a stockroom assistant—age 14.

1907 Begins to publish journalistic pieces.

1909 Foundation of the Irish Transport and General Workers' Union by Jim Larkin. O'Casey's association with the union begins soon after.

1913 Lock-out and strike; police violence. Subject matter for early O'Casey play, *The Harvest Festival* (rejected by the Abbey and never produced or published) and the later *Red Roses for Me*. Irish Citizen Army founded by the trade unions for protection.

1914 O'Casey secretary of the Irish Citizen Army, but resigns after several months in anger over ties with the middle-class Irish Volunteers. The Great War begins; Irish recruited by the British.

1916 The Easter Rising. O'Casey, disaffiliated with Irish

Citizen Army, remains a spectator. The next five years are of The Troubles, or Black-and-Tan War.

1918 Publication of *Songs of the Wren* and *The Story of Thomas Ashe*. Author's name: Sean O'Cathasaigh. First play, *The Frost in the Flower*, refused production by the St. Lawrence O'Toole Club as too controversial. Sister Isabella dies at the beginning of the year and Susan Casey dies toward the end: O'Casey now alone.

1919 *The Story of the Irish Citizen Army* by P. (sic) O'Cathasaigh published. Abbey rejects *The Frost in the Flower*, and in the next three years rejects *The Harvest Festival* and *The Crimson and the Tri-Colour* as well.

1921 Peace Treaty with Great Britain ends the Black-and-Tan War with the partition of Ireland; next two years are still violent as Republicans declare Civil War on the new Irish Free State government.

1923 *On the Run* accepted by the Abbey Theatre; title changed to *The Shadow of a Gunman* and successfully produced for a short run. O'Casey finances hardly affected; continues to work as a laborer. "Kathleen Listens In" apathetically received by Abbey audiences.

1924 *Juno and the Paycock* successfully produced at the Abbey. For the first time O'Casey begins a full-time career as a writer. One-act play, "Nannie's Night Out," also performed at the Abbey Theatre.

1925 *Juno* produced in London.

1926 *The Plough and the Stars* at the Abbey; riots on the fourth night and thereafter. O'Casey goes to

London to receive the Hawthornden Prize for *Juno*.

1927 Marries Irish actress Eileen Carey Reynolds in London.

1928 Rejection by the Abbey directorate of *The Silver Tassie*. O'Casey remains in England permanently and a running feud with the Abbey begins. Birth of son Breon.

1929 *The Silver Tassie* receives its premiere in London instead of Dublin.

1932 The Irish Academy formed by Shaw and Yeats; O'Casey and Joyce invited to join—both refuse.

1933 *Within the Gates* published.

1934 New York production of *Within the Gates*. O'Casey makes his first and only transatlantic journey to the United States. *Windfalls*, a collection of poems, stories, and plays, published.

1935 Abbey Theatre, hoping to perform *Within the Gates*, is offered *The Silver Tassie* by O'Casey. The directorate relent and *The Silver Tassie* receives its belated Dublin premiere.

1936 Birth of son Niall.

1937 *The Flying Wasp*, theatre criticism, published.

1939 Publication of *I Knock at the Door* ("Swift Glances Back At Things That Made Me"), first of six volumes of autobiography. Daughter Shivaun born. World War II begins; the O'Caseys leave London for Totnes, Devon.

1940 *The Star Turns Red* produced by left-wing theatre group in London. *Purple Dust* written.

1942 *Red Roses for Me* completed; produced the following year in Dublin. *Pictures in the Hallway* published.

1945 *Drums under the Window* published.

1946 *Oak Leaves and Lavender* published, but like many O'Casey plays does not receive immediate production.

1949 *Cock-a-Doodle Dandy* and *Inishfallen, Fare Thee Well* published. First two volumes of collected plays published.

1951 Publication of volumes three and four of *Collected Plays*.

1952 *Rose and Crown* published.

1954 *Sunset and Evening Star* published.

1955 *The Bishop's Bonfire* presented in Dublin; agitation and near riots.

1956 Publication of *The Green Crow* and *Mirror in My House*. Death of Niall O'Casey of leukemia.

1958 Dublin Theatre Festival scheduled to present *The Drums of Father Ned*, but the Archbishop of Dublin intervenes against O'Casey and Joyce. O'Casey declares war again against Dublin.

1961 Three plays (*Behind the Green Curtains*, "Figuro in the Night," and "The Moon Shines on Kylenamoe") published.

1964 O'Casey dies on September 18 of a heart attack in his home at 40 Trumlands Road, St. Marychurch, Torquay, Devon.

Introduction

The appearance of a new major playwright, one who combined artistic skill and popular appeal, would have been a welcome event at any time for the directors of Dublin's Abbey Theatre. In 1923, at a time of political turmoil, when the Abbey faced financial bankruptcy, it should have been greeted as a miracle. For Sean O'Casey the production of *The Shadow of a Gunman* and the emergence of an appreciative audience were no less miraculous, although his determination to become an Abbey playwright had prepared him for the success. He was 43 years old, had very little formal education, and had worked at various jobs as a manual laborer since adolescence, but too often subsisting as a member of Dublin's vast congregation of unemployed. Despite several minor publications (a history of the Irish Citizen Army for which he had served as Secretary prior to the Easter Rising, two volumes of "songs," and two political pamphlets), O'Casey was a complete unknown, whereas the Abbey was the single significant showcase for Irish drama. Getting past the guardians at the door (directors W. B. Yeats, Lennox Robinson, and Lady

Gregory) had proved no easy matter: only Lady Gregory offered very much encouragement to offset at least three rejections O'Casey had already suffered at their hands. Yeats maintained an Olympian preference for a rarified drama accessible only to an elite, and Robinson combined erratic judgment with a moralistic predilection. Lady Gregory found merit in the early efforts, praising the neophyte for his delineation of character, and quickly emerged as O'Casey's advocate as well as the object of his personal adoration. When the Abbey gates were slammed in O'Casey's face three years later —Lady Gregory proving too weak against the adamant attitudes of Yeats and Robinson—three major plays of the twentieth century had been produced by the Abbey and its reputation as Ireland's national theatre precariously preserved for the time being. And O'Casey was launched on very choppy waters as an established dramatist.

The three years were turbulent ones: Dublin audiences awakened to a new talent who had changed the nature of Irish drama from peasant comedies to a presumably realistic urban drama of Dublin slum life, tragicomedies which O'Casey himself labeled "tragedies." The scheduled run of only a week for *The Shadow of a Gunman* suggests the limited hopes of the directors in O'Casey's debut to the public, and the payment of a mere four pounds kept the new playwright at the pick and shovel for a while longer. In 1924, *Juno and the Paycock* reaffirmed the audience's enthusiasm for O'Caseyan drama, and the playwright went on to live by his pen thereafter. But a silent and sullen theatre reacted with apathy and incomprehension to one of the two one-act plays produced by O'Casey during this era, the political fantasy called "Kathleen Listens In," and it should have been apparent to all concerned that the playwright had no intention of contenting himself with a fixed and proven theatrical form—even his own. Nor was the newly remassed body of Dublin theatre-goers particularly adept at accepting the unfamiliar—even from the popular Sean O'Casey. Yet neither O'Casey nor the directorate was quite prepared for the outburst that greeted the third full-length play, *The Plough and the Stars*, in 1926. For the third time in a generation Dublin audiences rioted at the Abbey in reaction against inflammatory and controversial material on stage. Yeats, who had been the subject of the first riot and the staunch defender of Synge in the second, rushed back from London to embrace O'Casey and excoriate the rabble, appearing on stage in evening dress to deliver his denunciation: "You have disgraced yourselves again!" Never a lover of the common herd, and always hoping to antagonize the compact majority, he hailed O'Casey as a genius and called in the constabulary. Two years later, in firm compact with Robinson and with Lady Gregory's docile acquiescence, he flatly rejected O'Casey's next play, *The Silver Tassie*, earning a public blast from the enraged dramatist and assuring the complete exile of Sean O'Casey from his native Ireland.

The rejection of the play remains an almost inexplicable act of absurdity. One by one the directors came to regret their decision, making public but quiet confessions of error—Lady Gregory first; and several years later O'Casey and Yeats were playing croquet together. But O'Casey's exile from Ireland remained irrevocable. It is not really known whether he had actually considered transplanting himself in England when he left Dublin in 1926: he had gone over to attend the London production of *Juno* and receive the Hawthorndon award, and had fallen in love with and married Eileen Reynolds Carey, an Irish actress working on the London stage. Yeats's snub either fixed the mood of exile or added the final touch. Years later, in writing his autobiographical version of the event, O'Casey sounded resolute in his determination to make a conscious and definite break ("It was time for Sean to go. He had had enough of it. He would be no more of an exile in another land than he was in his own"), but it may have been a far more inadvertent decision based on a series of events, capped by the *Silver Tassie* disappointment. The Abbey could ill afford the loss of its major playwright (despite a recent Irish government subsidy), and has never fully recovered from the prolonged absence of O'Casey; and the playwright himself was divorced from both the source of his dramatic material and the theatre and company skilled in carrying out his artistic intentions. Of the two, O'Casey fared the better by far.

The reputation based on the first three full-length plays has remained as an ultimate verdict on Sean O'Casey, even when critics have failed to agree on the bases for their judgment. O'Casey himself cautioned against viewing the plays as photographic realism. (The dramatist's detractors have often dismissed them as only that, while several of his defenders have admired the plays for just that quality.) He went on in exile to quadruple the body of his dramatic output, experimenting often in expressionistic and other non-realistic techniques, and maintaining throughout that the spirit of such experimentation was already operative in the Dublin plays. Many commentators have also assumed that these early plays were essentially formless, an almost accidental throwing together of a variety of characters who play out their individual slices of life on O'Casey's stage: O'Casey has therefore been credited with utilizing a fortuitously free-form drama, and has also been criticized for careless formlessness. Eventually a handful of critics appeared who praised the dramatist for the intuitive sense of stagecraft which made these same plays so eminently successful. Irish commentators, particularly of the playwright's own generation, have mostly bemoaned the loss of O'Casey's talent once he left his homeland and attempted to ape the questionable ventures of continental playwrights; their familiar thesis is that an Irish writer destroys himself when he wanders off the native footpath and becomes prey to "foreign" influences. O'Casey reacted with a quick temper to such attitudes, insisting that his hand remained firm in his execution of his craft. Certainly his subject matter remained almost exclusively Irish, with only one or two exceptions, and for over thirty years he kept in touch with political and social changes in Ireland, mirroring them in his new plays and remaining a persistent critic of essential elements of Irish life under the Republic.

O'Casey also defended the efficacy of his experimental

methods, often pointing to his most recent work as his best. He eventually decided upon *Cock-a-Doodle Dandy*, a product of the mid-1940s, as his finest play. It is characteristic of an artist to defend his later unproved efforts at the expense of his earlier established pieces, and O'Casey was eventually fortunate that several critics enlisted themselves on his side: even if they have not succeeded in their efforts against the tide to establish the later plays as O'Casey's best, they have at least focused expert attention on the late plays and contributed valuable analyses of them. Critical acclaim, whether of the later part of the canon or of the early Dublin dramas, has hardly been enough to offset O'Casey's failure to receive adequate productions in London and New York (where any play written in English must survive and be revived for any definitive judgment to be possible). O'Casey's feud with the Abbey (particularly the 1958 rejection of *The Drums of Father Ned*) for a time kept all O'Casey plays off the boards in Ireland; at other times the Abbey has returned over and over to the three major plays. No other playwright but O'Casey can guarantee a full house in Dublin, and the inauguration of the new Abbey playhouse in 1966 featured *The Plough and the Stars*. The dearth of London or New York productions of so well-known a writer as O'Casey has been credited to many things: lack of acting skill in handling Irish dialect or the subtlety of O'Caseyan techniques; elaborate stagecraft demands made by a dramatist writing without access to immediate production; the shifting of genres within a single play, confusing audiences conditioned to a single sustained tone in their dramatic fare. Despite the advocacy of such entrenched theatre arbiters as George Jean Nathan and Brooks Atkinson, the general verdict has been that O'Casey's plays were too difficult for production.

The difficulty began with *The Silver Tassie*, particularly the highly expressionistic second act that so disturbed W. B. Yeats and delighted G. B. Shaw (who pronounced it a phantasmagoria). Yeats's objections are mystifying. O'Casey was quick to assume that Lennox Robinson was prejudiced against him because of the audacious nature of *The Plough*, but Yeats was a dramatist committed to poetic experimentation in the theatre and should logically have preferred the method apparent in *The Tassie* over the basically naturalistic techniques of the previous O'Casey plays. It was expressionism in particular that O'Casey espoused in the 1930s from his London place of exile: *Within the Gates* (1934) depends throughout its four acts on verse choruses, archetypal characters without individualized identities, seasons and time of day that change with each act, and even transformations that take place in the statue which dominates the stage. Also, political statement—present in oblique ways in the Dublin plays (but sufficiently direct to offend in *The Plough* and to stultify in "Kathleen")—became a dominant aspect with the sounding of the anti-war theme in *The Tassie*. *The Star Turns Red* (1939), by consensus O'Casey's worst play because of its propagandistic heavyhandedness, focused attention on a death struggle between Fascists and Communists in a Dublin of the future, and

Oak Leaves and Lavender (1947) celebrated the heroism of a Communist Irishman fighting for Britain in
World War II against German Nazism. In the non-
Communist world these two plays have virtually disappeared from serious consideration, handled only by
the most enthusiastic of O'Caseyans, and even then with
a touch of embarrassment.

It is a 1940 comedy, *Purple Dust*, that serves as an
introduction to the later O'Casey style, the plays of
comic fantasy. This remained the essential vein of his
dramatic work until his death almost 25 years later,
interrupted occasionally by such propaganda pieces as
Oak Leaves and by his most autobiographic statement
in drama, *Red Roses for Me* (1942). The latter exists
for many as a unique piece of O'Caseyana, a personal,
poetic, and tender statement from the dramatist, re-
calling the power of his naturalistic efforts of the 20s,
but blending these with touches of fantasy and expressionistic poetry in the third act, and incorporating
some of O'Casey's finest comic elements. The playwright had begun to write his autobiography in the
late 30s, the six volumes of which began to appear in
1940 (*I Knock at the Door*). The succession of these
books paralleled O'Casey's succession of plays through
the 40s and 50s, and having depicted his Dublin childhood in the first and then the second volume (*Pictures
in the Hallway*, 1942), O'Casey went on to portray his
young manhood in both volume three, *Drums under
the Window* (1946) and in *Red Roses*, working on the
two versions simultaneously. The Johnny Casside of the
autobiography and the Ayamonn Breydon of the play

fuse into a single figure, the young O'Casey of the early years of the century. The three later volumes, *Inishfallen, Fare Thee Well* (1948), *Rose and Crown* (1952), and *Sunset and Evening Star* (1954), depict the playwright from his earliest efforts through his life of exile in England, and combine the caustic literary and political commentary that O'Casey had begun to publish in the 30s. Such volumes as *The Flying Wasp* (1937), *The Green Crow* (1956), and *Under a Colored Cap* (1962) provided periodic outlets for the collected opinions of O'Casey the critic, the titles reflecting the sting, the caw, and the witty sense of his singular observations. Also felicitous is editor Ronald Ayling's title for a posthumous collection of periodical pieces: *Blasts and Benediction* (1967).

The O'Casey of the *Purple Dust* vein cast a cold eye on the paralysis of rural Ireland (abandoning the Dublin urban scene in which he had lived for 46 years for the small town, the village, and the farm community in which social change was even slower in making itself felt than in the capital city). Here he uncovered the dead hand of the parish priest, the self-aggrandizing grasp of the new Irish landowners, and the occasional defiant fist of a socially aware rebel. The landlords are still British in the 1940 "wayward comedy," but thereafter in *Cock-a-Doodle Dandy* (1949), *The Bishop's Bonfire* (1955), and *The Drums of Father Ned* (1958) they are Irish parvenus, graduated to councillors and mayors and elected as papal counts. Hand in glove with the bigoted clergy, they keep a tight grip on the politics, economy, mores, and morality of their petty fiefdoms, attempting to stem the natural tide of freedom, love, rebellion, and life itself. O'Casey's young people often demand the right to shape their own futures, for romantic love and passion, for song and dance and an open investigation of all closed issues, and when denied these rights by parent and priest they opt for emigration to England rather than atrophy in Ireland. In the rare event of victory over the forces of the dead past, they jauntily take command of their world, leaving the rulers of the old society to atrophy. O'Casey's technique in these late comedies parallels that of the Dublin plays in their blend of the tragic and the pathetic with the wildly comic, but with strong elements of fantasy for leavening. Supernatural birds, superhuman heroes, mysterious priests who stir the youth to rebellion—all embodiments of the Life Force—take command in the more optimistic of the plays (*Purple Dust, The Drums of Father Ned*, and the shorter "Figuro in the Night") and usher in the O'Caseyan future. But in the more somber dramas, despite the many flashes of hilarity and song, the mood of bitterness predominates, and the fallen angels retreat, refusing to serve the fierce god and tyrannical master, often leaving behind those of their fellows who cannot muster the courage to take a stand: *Cock-a-Doodle Dandy, The Bishop's Bonfire*, and O'Casey's last full-length play, *Behind the Green Curtains* (1961).

Although he did not follow chronological order in the composition of these plays, many of O'Casey's dramas concern some of the most important political events in Irish and European history during O'Casey's lifetime. His individual attitudes dominate the action of these theatrical recreations, but every important facet of twentieth-century history is mirrored here, as well as in the six autobiographies collected in 1956 under the cumulative title of *Mirror in My House*. The 1913 Transport Workers Strike and Lockout, which established Jim Larkin as the leader of the Irish labor movement, provides the setting and action of *Red Roses for Me*, a fictionalized version of that event but specifically dedicated to the men and women who participated in it. A year later the Great War began, and Irish soldiers were recruited for the British Army to fight in France: O'Casey's play *The Silver Tassie* focused on three such soldiers, their roles in the war and their return to Dublin, one paralyzed from the waist down, the second blinded, and the third triumphant and bemedaled, claiming all the spoils of victory. The Easter Rising in 1916 is depicted in the last two acts of *The Plough and the Stars*, the first two having established the diverse attitudes and personalities of the participants, the brave and the cowardly, the nationalists and the pro-British, the combatants and the civilians, supporters, hecklers, looters, and begrieved. The quelling of the insurrection changed the nature of the conflict from open warfare to guerrilla activities employed by the I. R. A. against the British, and the retaliation which employed such professional killers as the Black and Tans and the Auxies; this period of the Troubles provides the background for *The Shadow of a Gunman*, the scene of a raid on a tenement building in which Mills bombs have been hidden by a gunman on the run.

Nor did the establishment of an Irish Free State of the 26 southern counties bring peace: Civil War between the Free Staters who accepted the compromise and Republican diehards who demanded total victory continued the reign of terror, and O'Casey's *Juno and the Paycock* depicts the senseless horror of the internecine conflict; a twice-wounded hero turns coward and traitor and is executed by his former comrades, his mother echoing the grief of her neighbor, whose dead son had been the victim of his treachery.

Contemporary Irish history has remained rather tame and uneventful since the end of the Civil War, but O'Casey's focus remained political. The economic depression of the 1930s made itself felt in England, and O'Casey chose London's Hyde Park as the scene of his depression play *Within the Gates*, where the threnody of the Down-and-Out sends chills of horror through the denizens of the park. The Spanish Civil War of 1936 drew firm battlelines between the Left and the Right, threatening to diminish the politics of the center to complete insignificance. Sean O'Casey identified himself strongly with the death-struggle of the Left, and although *The Star Turns Red* does not actually depict the Spanish struggle, it fantasizes it into an epic conflict set in the future in O'Casey's Dublin, where the dominant forces of capitalism, fascism, and the Church are threatened at last by militant labor, led by a Red Jim modeled after Larkin and much larger than life-size. *The Star* was written during the waning days of the Civil War, while the Popular Front was facing imminent defeat, but O'Casey's political fantasy predicted eventual victory for those losing defenders of the left-wing Republic.

During the opening stages of World War II, while Churchill's Britain opposed Hitler's Germany, O'Casey refrained from dramatic commitment. Instead he composed his comedy of two British Blimp-figures playing rural squire in the newly liberated Ireland. Written while a resident in England, *Purple Dust* angered British critics who saw it as an unfair attack on the beleaguered English during their darkest hour. O'Casey did in fact go on to write his celebration of English courage during the Battle of Britain, but only after the war was enlarged to include the Soviet Union as England's ally—and his central hero was the Irish Communist R.A.F. pilot. As in each of the previous instances, the playwright's viewpoint was uniquely his own, shaped by his basic humanitarian vision that saw the effects of war primarily upon its victims, by his basically pacifistic attitude which was nonetheless overturned when certain ideals had to be fought for, and by his omnipresent belief in the efficacy of a socialist future that took precedence over all other concerns. After World War II O'Casey returned his focus to the Ireland he had fled, carefully watching the signals from across the Irish Sea which told him of movements for change within the new theocracy and repressive battles being fought by the new rulers for continued dominance over the moral thinking of the nation. His later comic-fantasies, exultant, bitter and bitter-sweet, depicted the 1940s and 50s in Ireland, or at least O'Casey's surmise of the tenor of the times.

Sean O'Casey's life, a span of 84 years from 1880 to 1964, provides a microcosm of Irish events from the days of Parnell—his ascendency and fall, his death and its aftermath are central to the opening volumes of the O'Casey autobiographies—through the reign of Eamon de Valera, the guiding spirit of the Ireland examined in the comic fantasies. In addition O'Casey lived the varied life of a middle-class child, an impoverished adolescent and young adult, a common laborer (and as often as not an unemployed one), a celebrated Dublin playwright (and a controversial one), an exile in England with an international reputation, largely unhonored in his native Ireland. He concerned himself and his art intimately with Irish life and the life of the world, permanently capturing in his plays and autobiographies the world he knew. His output includes 22 published plays, the six volumes of "backward glances at things that made me," and numerous essays and stories and songs, all stamped by the individuality of his own personality and an exciting interest in the variety of the tricks of the trade. He learned his craft from such diverse sources as Shakespeare and Boucicault, Shaw and the Bible, learning for himself to handle the traditional devices of that craft while insisting upon an open spirit of experimentation throughout. Between Synge on one end of the chronological spectrum and a yawning void on the other, Sean O'Casey stands as Irish drama almost by himself—and one of the best dramatists writing in the English language in his time in any country. His imperfections were enormous. He insisted upon utilizing melodrama, and he dangerously juggled genres; he was heavyhanded in his diction, propagandistic with a vengeance, and even derivative. He had faults enough to demolish any other writer—yet he mastered his art, polished his techniques, took his chances, and survived his mistakes, rarely concentrating them to any great extent. He emerged with a voice of his own, a style of his own, and a body of artistic work that reflected his personality and thinking with flair and color. The process that resulted in the making of a dramatist succeeded in producing a distinctively unusual one.

1
O'Casey in the Works

Reliable as literary art O'Casey's autobiographic *Mirror* is tendentious as literal biography. Not that the writer was contemptuous of accurate reportage (he maintained an unusual respect for the profession of the honest journalist), but more than one life was being recorded in the six volumes of personal recollections. *Mirror in My House* is both a portrait of the artist (O'Casey himself) and a portrait of *an* artist (a fictional John-Johnny-Sean Casside who contains multitudes), yet it is the unrelenting single vision of a particular personality with a fixed point of view. Faithful to chronology as a sequence, it is cavalier with actual dates: one tells time by noting the historical event in the background, since calendar and clock are rarely present. As such it is the portrait of two worlds: Dublin between the 1880s and 1920s, and several decades thereafter of exile outside Dublin. Even so absolute a point of departure as the author's date of birth, March 30, 1880, is transformed into once-upon-a-time: "In Dublin, sometime in the early eighties, on the last day of the month of March . . ."

It was no easy matter for John Casey to be born and to grow up to become Sean O'Casey. Dublin at the time, hailed as the second city of the British Empire and the seventh city of Christendom, was first in infant mortality, a "fact" never stated in *I Knock at the Door* but dramatically symbolized: two previous male children named John had been born to the Cassides and both had died. It is the death of the second John that is depicted in the opening chapter—a frantic mother taking the infant to a hospital, moving through stalled traffic in the wake of a procession for Charles Stewart Parnell, and having the child die of croup in her arms waiting for a doctor. The father is understandably leery of the risk of naming still a third son John, but the mother remains firm and defiant in her insistence that this child shall live. Weak and small, troubled from an early age with painfully diseased eyes that prevented formal schooling, the child survived—a statistical anomaly. Disease, illness, sudden death, poverty, hardship, disadvantage—these persist as the thematic structures of the world O'Casey artistically re-created from life around him and from aspects of his own life. Occasionally a Dublin critic, defensive of his city and incensed by O'Casey's grim portraiture, will insist that the playwright's childhood had not actually been so poverty-ridden as he shows Johnny Casside's to be. Nevertheless, O'Casey's lies have the truth of fictional reality.

O'Casey's roots are admittedly middle-class; his allegiance to and concern with the working class derive

from ideological choice and the quick demoralization of his family's economic position. His father, Michael Casey, came from Limerick, a devout Protestant disturbed by the Catholic-Protestant split within his family. As a member of the "ascendant" Protestant minority in Ireland he should logically have been a part of the social and economic elite, but he preferred dedicating himself to employment by charitable organizations at a meager salary, establishing himself and his family in a shabby genteel residence only slightly better than the tenements later depicted in his son's plays. His avid reading and concern with education mark him as decidedly superior to his environment and provided a legacy for Sean to offset the effects of the family's financial decline. Michael Casey's death when his youngest son was still a child began the serious progress of that decline, although there were then four older siblings to serve as breadwinners. Marriage and mindless military careers, however, decimated their ranks, and the family of three watched the disappearance of the last brake to the skid into poverty. Subsequent brutalization of the older children by Army life and marriage and childbearing, by the combined onslaught of various environmental and personal factors, further deteriorated an already hopeless situation. Sean and his mother now settled down to relentless poverty. He was soon a conscript to child labor and later to menial jobs that permanently fixed his attitudes and provided his basic subject matter.

O'Casey's Dublin is geographically only the segment of the city north of the Liffey River, separated by worlds from the elegant and fashionable squares of the south-eastern portion. He was born on Dorset Street and baptized in the parish church of St. Mary's on Mary Street, living all of his Dublin days in that general area. Even those structures that were still respectable at the time of his birth, especially the Georgian houses of the late eighteenth century, soon became overcrowded tenements by the end of the nineteenth century. With the death of his mother in 1918 O'Casey abandoned the last of the "parental" dwellings, those two-room flats that set the stage in *Juno, The Plough, The Tassie,* and *Red Roses*: now on his own he moved into equivalent dwellings, sharing a room with a peddler on Mountjoy Square and living alone on North Circular Road thereafter. The one-room setting for *The Gunman* is located by the author on "Hilljoy Square," where peddler Seumas Shields recaptures the essence of O'Casey's flatmate and Donal Davoren is a caricature of the writer himself. (The house at 422 North Circular Road, where O'Casey wrote most of his early successes, now bears a plaque commemorating his residence there.) The world of O'Casey's Dublin is far removed from the Merrion Square where Yeats lived and wrote, and O'Casey recalls with some bitterness that he was never invited as a guest into the "Big Houses" of Merrion Square, even when he was the most talked about dramatist in Dublin. Yet the smaller we draw the circle around the essential Dublin that was O'Casey's, the more monumental that world looms as a microcosm of a much larger universe.

If Donal Davoren in O'Casey's first stage success is

a portrait of the artist as a young man, it is more caricature than portraiture. O'Casey's intention, however, was to stay close to familiar material from life in setting the scene and establishing the situation: thereafter he reworked his characters to serve his dramatic purposes. Like the younger Sean, Donal is a would-be poet living in a tenement, but it is apparent that the effete Donal never wielded a pick or worked on the railroad. As a poet he is completely uninterested in the lives around him, while the budding playwright listened avidly to his fellow slumdwellers and took notes of their speech. Nor could Donal's deception—allowing the impressed neighbors to believe that he is an anti-British gunman in hiding—ever have appealed to the man of self-lacerating honesty, who was also too much aware of the political situation occurring around him not to have seen the danger of maintaining such a pretension. O'Casey's own bravery has always been very much in question, particularly by the Irish patriot who gauges valor by determining whether you were "out in '16": O'Casey had already turned his back on the nationalistic movement by the time of the Easter Rising of 1916, over a political squabble within the Irish Citizen Army, and remained an interested bystander during the Troubles and the Civil War. His motives were ideological—the nationalistic movement seemed destined to establish the rule of the Irish middle class, rather than aid the downtrodden proletariat; his prognosis has been verified by history, but he was unashamedly candid in his frequent comment that he was grateful to have avoided risking the red badge of

courage. Donal's cowardice may well mirror his creator's, but the kind of courage that is lifelong personal
integrity cannot be taken away from O'Casey.

The story of the raid by British "shock troops" upon
a tenement building in which a gunman was allegedly
lodged is recounted twice by Sean O'Casey, fictionally
in *The Shadow of a Gunman* and autobiographically
in a chapter of *Inishfallen, Fare Thee Well* titled "The
Raid." In the play a lovely young neighbor named
Minnie Powell becomes enamored of Donal, crediting
him with the distinction of being a gunman and with
the attributes of an educated and refined poet. When
Donal and Seumas belatedly inspect the bag left by a
peddler named Maguire (who had been killed that
day in an ambush, Maguire having been an actual
gunman), they discover Mills bombs. But only the
presence of the Auxies in the tenement had alerted
them to search the bag—and now it is too late. Donal
and Seumas become interchangeable in their cowardly
terror, while Minnie (capable of personal bravery and
in love with Donal) takes the bag of bombs into her
room, hoping that a woman will not be carefully
searched, but determined to take her chances nonetheless. When Minnie is arrested, defiantly shouting
"Up the Republic," and subsequently killed in an ambush outside the building, Seumas is relieved and contemptuous of her, but Donal is capable of a moment
of self-awareness:

> It's terrible to think that little Minnie is dead, but it's
> still more terrible to think that Davoren and Shields
> are alive! Oh, Donal Davoren, shame is your portion

now till the silver cord is loosened and the golden bowl be broken. Oh, Davoren, Donal Davoren, poet and poltroon, poltroon and poet!

Davoren is not the only character in the play to carry aspects of the playwright onto the stage: even Seumas Shields, although patently modeled after Michael Mullen, contains O'Casey characteristics. His negative aspects O'Casey would certainly not take credit for: he is comically lazy, ignorantly religious, and dogmatically superstitious. (Still in bed past noon he berates Maguire for being too lazy to get up early enough to keep an appointment, claims to be a daily communicant although he has obviously missed Mass, glories in Shelley being tortured in hell, and insists that the raid and Minnie's death resulted from mysterious tappings he had heard on the wall.) But there are moments in *The Gunman* when the comic Seumas almost steals the play for himself. Davoren as protagonist is of course only a shadow of a gunman, and not much more of a real poet or a real man, and Seumas scores often at his expense. His knowledge of Greek mythology and of literature is surprising for a superstition-ridden notions-seller; he manages to spot every one of Donal's quotations (atheistic Shelley included) and quotes Shakespeare with citations of chapter and verse. At times he even serves as the author's spokesman, attempting to correct Donal's arrogantly narrow concept of aesthetics:

I don't profess to know much about poetry—about poetry —I don't know much about the pearly glint of the morning dew, or the damask sweetness of the rare wild rose,

or the subtle greenness of the serpent's eye—but I think
a poet's claim to greatness depends upon his power to
put passion in the common people.

This is O'Casey talking, while Shields's insistence that
"I knew things ud go wrong when I missed Mass this
mornin'" is the other end of the spectrum.

In "The Raid" the protagonist is Sean Casside, living
alone in a tenement room when the Tans invade. He
too is the object of romantic interest, although he has
made no pretense to being a gunman, nor has he
flaunted himself as a poet. But instead of the slow
developing of romance that takes place in the play,
the situation here is a bit more turbulent: a somewhat
timid Sean is in the process of being seduced by a brazen
and unsubtle Mrs. Ballynoy, whose husband is presumably away. She enters Sean's room in scanty nightclothes after the raid, and leaps into his bed pretending
fright. The return of the Tans interrupts the im-
promptu seduction, and this time they find Mr. Ballynoy
and his arms in a shed behind the house. The cuck-
olded husband is dragged away, like Minnie shouting
his defiant "Up th' Republic!" Here as in *The Gunman*
O'Casey demonstrates his fascination with the concept
that heroism is found in the most unlikely places, in
a wisp of a girl like Minnie, a peddler like Maguire, a
cuckold like Charlie Ballynoy. It was a theme that he
went on to develop in many of his works.

O'Casey gave to his play *The Shadow of a Gunman*
the designation of "a tragedy," presumably because of
the death of Minnie Powell, a relatively minor character. His next play, *Juno and the Paycock*, is also termed

a tragedy, again because one of the lesser characters, Johnny Boyle, is killed. Johnny is a portrait of Sean O'Casey as he might have been had he continued in his participation in the Irish Citizen Army and gone "out in '16." The young Boyle had been little more than a child at the time, but sustained serious wounds, and we now see him during the Civil War cowering at home in abject terror. Twice a hero (hit in the hip by a bullet during the Easter Rising, he went on to fight against the Free State and had his arm shattered by a bomb), he is now a coward. A patriot beyond the call of duty, he has now betrayed a fellow Republican, his neighbor Robbie Tancred, and fears reprisal. Such reversals of character may seem mysterious and difficult for a playwright to carry off, but they are at the core of O'Casey's technique as a dramatist and central to his view of life: unexpected heroism from some, inexplicable cowardice from others. Johnny is dragged off to be shot by the I.R.A., and it is now his mother's turn to wail in sorrow as Mrs. Tancred had done.

By the time he began to write plays O'Casey was already a dedicated socialist, but the early tenement plays are devoid of propagandistic evidence. He concentrated on real events, their complexities and their multiple effects on the people he knew, rarely showing his hand to his audience. (The same Dubliners who were being dissected and lampooned in these comic tragedies sat in the theatre and roared at themselves, until the full brunt of O'Casey's satire struck home in *The Plough and the Stars*.) Laughing at himself was as important to the dramatist as mocking others, and in both *Juno* and *The Plough* he was capable of a satiric caricature of rather unlovely socialists. In the first a unionist named Jerry Devine has been courting Johnny's sister Mary, holding out the possibility that he will become a Union secretary and marry her. But despite her own trade union loyalties—she is out on strike as the play opens—Mary has set her sights on a bourgeois schoolteacher named Charlie Bentham. She turns her back on Jerry, only to find herself abandoned by Bentham and pregnant by him. Magnanimous Jerry offers to take her back, but quickly rescinds his offer when he learns to his horror that she is pregnant. Having made grandiose statements like "With Labour, Mary, humanity is above everything; we are the leaders in the fight for a new life," he now backs toward the door, denounced by Mary: "your humanity is just as narrow as the humanity of the others." In *The Plough* Jerry's successor is a young Marxist known as the Covey, whose offensiveness is marked by his dogmatism and querulousness. He is forever attempting to foist revolutionary literature upon anyone he suspects might be receptive and constantly goes out of his way to bait the foolish old Uncle Peter. He is never afforded the opportunity of Jerry Devine's kind of betrayal, but has the rug pulled from under him by an enterprising prostitute named Rosie Redmond. When everyone else is occupied by the political rally, Rosie and the Covey find themselves alone in the pub. She sizes him up as a potential customer, but he naively assumes that she is interested in his pronouncements on "conthrol o' th' means o' production, rates of exchange, an' th' means of disthribution." Rosie feigns interest long enough to make her intentions clear—to the utter horror of the young prude. Loving humanity in the abstract, the Jerry Devines and the Coveys fail as human beings by being unable to respond humanely to the individual people around them.

Yet satire was not the only means employed by O'Casey to criticize those who shared his ideas but lacked breadth and scope in their approach to life. In *Within the Gates* he presents a tender portrayal of Ned, whom he most often identifies expressionistically as the Atheist. There is little doubt that O'Casey identifies with him and commends him in many ways as a fine person: it is the Atheist who had served as a foster-father to the fatherless heroine of the play and commiserates with her situation but finds himself no longer able to do anything further to help Jannice. He voices O'Casey's own annoyance with ignorance and superstition and argues against the fears of hell. When Jannice reveals to him the fearful dreams she has, he is "scornful and angry": "The hell en' red-fire for ever talk of the nuns! They frame the world en' fill life with it, till we eat, sleep, work, en' play for ever in the smoke of hell!" Yet there is a flaw in the Atheist that his young friend the Dreamer is quick to discover: when Ned boasts that he delivered Jannice from the Church and urged her to read Thomas Paine, the Dreamer asks, "And did you bring her into touch with song?" "Song? Oh, I had no time for song!", Ned replies. But the Dreamer is adamant in his reproof:

> You led her from one darkness into another, man. . . . Will none of you ever guess that man can study man, or worship God, in dance and song and story! [*Appealingly*] Ah, Ned, if you could but see her with the eyes of youth, you would not let her live so lonely.

It is the Dreamer who is O'Casey's spokesman and protagonist, a projection of himself and his ideals. The Atheist is quick to learn from his younger friend, and attempts to dissuade Jannice from despair, from joining the ranks of the Down-and-Out as the Bishop (her actual father) encourages her to do:

> Jannice, stand firm, and remember that you are the bride of the Dreamer. Tell him that the world shall be, not what his God wills, but what fighting man can make it. Tell him you have given life a dance and the Dreamer has given life a song!

The Dreamer says yes to life without hedging. He writes poems—and sells them in order to live and to support Jannice; he amorously pursues Jannice—but with no romantic illusions of love for eternity or even a lifetime. He is the first of O'Casey's self-idealized heroes, redeemed by his existence in the drama as a symbolic entity rather than as a representational individual. In *The Star Turns Red* O'Casey again attempted to create a hero whose single-faceted aspects are offset by his symbolic role, but Jack is mired to a greater extent in the naturalistic elements of an otherwise expressionistic drama. He plays the "Internationale" on the cornet, irritates his old parents with his Communist loyalties, delivers himself of slogans and pronouncements, and dies heroically for a cause. Jack is too much involved in the actual plot of the play: he is too ineffectual to be able to prevent the Saffron Shirts from taking Julia out to be whipped or to prevent her father from being killed by their Leader. It is the larger-than-lifesized Union leader, Red Jim, who is credited with the action necessary to effect change. He defeats the corrupt leadership of his Union, reforms his drunken lieutenant, prevents the Purple Priest from claiming the body of Julia's father, and engineers the victory over the forces of reaction. Wooden as he is, Jack is nonetheless capable of an occasional touch that gives him a momentary dimension. When his old mother envisions a star on the eastern horizon, her husband and Julia are disappointed to realize that it is only the shopworn Star of Bethlehem that she sees; but atheistic Jack is dreamer enough to share her dream and is the only one to show an interest in it: "So it shone when it led the kings; so shall it not shine when it leads the people. It leads no more, and never shall till its silver turns to red."

The young Communist hero becomes a set figure in the later plays, his credibility often depending upon personal factors that breathe life into him. No sooner had O'Casey created the Jack of *The Star* than he turned his attention to another Jack, a foreman stonemason named O'Killigain in *Purple Dust*. He is far

more human than his predecessor and almost as monumental as Red Jim, but he functions within a relatively nonpolitical story and is three-dimensional. Like
the Dreamer his primary characteristic is as a lover,
as he woos away the beautiful Irish mistress of his
stodgy English employer. His political credentials are
very much in order—he fought on the side of the
Loyalists in the Spanish Civil War and has a scar on
his arm to show for it. Also, he is outspoken in front
of everyone, and we learn that he is "for ever fillin'
the place with reckless talk against the composure of
the Church in the midst of the way things are now"
and that "Canon Chreehewel's mad to dhrive him
outa th' place, with all who hear him." His one ally
is Philib O'Dempsey, the "2nd workman," a strange
and mystical man with a vast fund of Irish folklore.
Both are openly defiant of the two Englishmen whose
crumbling Tudor mansion they have been hired to
resurrect, and no efforts on the part of Stoke and Poges
to get "round" them ever succeeds. O'Killigain and
O'Dempsey prophesy the toppling ruin of the decayed
house on the heads of the London businessmen who
are naively attempting to shore up the vestiges of the
past. O'Dempsey predicts the coming of the Flood,
and while his foreman is luring Avril away from Stoke,
he lures Poges's mistress Souhaun away with him:
"Come, then, an' abide with the men o' th' wide
wathers, who can go off in a tiny curragh o' thought
to the New Island with th' outgoin' tide, an' come
back be th' same tide sweepin' in again!" While Stoke
and Poges and their servile entourage seek refuge in
the higher stories of the shaky mansion, the lovers

gallop off on horseback into the hills. The Flood that sweeps in to wash away the purple dust is far more effective symbolism for the O'Casey revolution than the Red Star and workers' victory of a starry future, and Jack O'Killigain and Philib O'Dempsey emerge from O'Casey's canon as two of his most poetic depictions.

There are vestiges of O'Killigain's robust humor and O'Dempsey's romantic dreaminess in Drishogue O'Morrigun of *Oak Leaves and Lavender*, but not quite enough. His love affair with Monica is far more sensual than that of Jack and Julia, nor is Drishogue as superhumanly even-tempered in the face of his opposition. The World War II situation here lends greater credence to the events of the play, in comparison to a revolution taking place when "the star turns red." Drishogue is a Communist ("Over in the east, the people took their first fine step forward, and they look over the rim of the world now"), an R.A.F. pilot in the war against Nazism ("Oh, how I long to take the sky by storm!"), and an eager lover ("We'll pull aside shy-buttoned bodice, to glimpse fair perfection beneath"), yet he has that touch of the dreamer that allows him to smell the lavender and hear the music that foreshadow death. Embracing life he is nonetheless unafraid of dying:

> And death is but a part of life, my friend. Dying, we shall not feel lonely, for the great cloud of witnesses who die will all be young. If death be the end, then there is nothing; if it be but a passage from one place to another, then we shall mingle with a great, gay crowd!

Drishogue is intended to be triumphant in everything,

in love and in friendship, in his political debate with the anti-Soviet Deeda Tutting (so that even his father, who is far too traditional to accept his radical viewpoint, joins him in reacting against her insidious attacks), and in his death in the air. His death is reported—as Jack's had been—and Monica mourns for him without losing the resolute determination that he had taught her. She reveals that she carries Drishogue's child and that they had had a registry marriage; the spirit of Drishogue O'Morrigun rises above the circumstances of his physical death and the chaos of Britain at war.

Those warriors who die in battle are comparably more fortunate than those who return. O'Casey had earlier dealt with the first World War in *The Silver Tassie*, focusing on football hero Harry Heegan coming off the field in exultant triumph with the tassie in tow and the adoring Jessie Taite in his arms. But Harry returning from the battlefield is a helpless cripple from the waist down, violently bitter about the loss of his legs and the defection of Jessie to his friend. Equally bitter is the Manus Moanroe who served in the R.A.F. in the second World War. Although sound in body he is sick in his soul, coming back in *The Bishop's Bonfire* to a provinicial Irish town not one jot the better than it had ever been. Independence from Great Britain has only brought the petty landlord into local power, abetted by the parish priest: together they maintain their moralistic stranglehold on Ballyoonagh, Councillor Reiligan having been made a papal count and Canon Burren advanced to

Monsignor. Manus is a spoiled priest in love with
Reiligan's daughter Foorawn, who has dedicated her
life to the Church. His fury reaches boiling level in
the last act, when he has decided to escape from the
dead town and is confronted by Foorawn as he is
stealing her church money. His denunciation is all-
inclusive:

> The fraud of clericals forbidding drink in the dance
> halls, though here, in Ballyoonagh, drinkers from Reili-
> gan's tavern go to the dance hall to dance, and dancers
> from Reiligan's dance halls go to Reiligan's tavern to
> drink; the fraud of Reiligan's town stores where there's
> nothing in spirit or manner to show that life's more
> than meat, and the body than raiment; the fraud of
> his mean meadows where his bunchy cattle low their
> woe to God for want of grass; the fraud of his shirt
> factory where girls work but to earn enough to leave
> the land, and where there's more melody in the heart
> of a machine than in the heart of its minder.

When Foorawn adamantly refuses to allow Manus
to steal the money he feels is rightfully his and begins
to telephone the police, Manus shoots her. Realizing
that she is dying, Foorawn allows herself to admit her
love for Manus and writes a suicide note.

The Bishop's Bonfire is O'Casey's bitterest comedy,
a drama he subtitled "A Sad Play within the Tune of
a Polka." Writing from across the Irish Sea he envisioned himself as a young Manus attempting to cope
with the bigotry and life-destroying emptiness of the
new Irish Republic. The exile he had chosen for
himself is often the only solution he offers for those
characters he admires, those who have still a spark of

life in them that they hope to keep from extinction. In his last play, written when he was 80, his hero is again the Irish Communist. ("You see, I happen to be a Red," Martin Boeman acknowledges to the shocked Reena.) Boeman has the self-assurance with which O'Casey often endows those characters who are skilled craftsmen. Like O'Killigain and Manus Moanroe, he is a foreman praised and valued by his employer, Dennis Chatastray, but except to enrage the ignorant gosoons with his radical ideas, Martin Boeman tends to remain in the background as much as possible. *Behind the Green Curtains* develops into the final scene as a drama centering on Chatastray and Reena: they are part of a group that comes to the Protestant church where a noted literary figure is lying in state. The Catholics are warned against entering the church, although Boeman goads them on with delight. Chatastray is unable to bring himself to defy the ban broadcast from the Archbishop's Palace, but Reena intrepidly enters. She is reprimanded for her defiance, and soon forms a romantic attachment with Dennis Chatastray—there is a chance that together they can stand up to the dead hand of narrow-minded authority. Boeman watches at a distance, offering his encouragement and assistance, but Chatastray proves too weak and joins the others in the anti-Communist demonstration. The shy Boeman is left with Reena, whose kisses embolden him so that he sweeps her up in his arms and carries her off to England.

The young Sean Casside of the autobiographies is also depicted as a shy lover enlivened by bolder women. In *I Knock at the Door* as a young boy he steals his first kiss from Jennie Clitheroe and sees the gesture as an initiation into the adult world; in *Pictures in the Hallway* a young Alice entices the feverish Johnny into his first affair in "some grassy nook" and Daisy Battles lures him into her bed; and in *Inishfallen* it is Mrs. Ballynoy who enters his dark room. Neither the Dreamer nor Jack O'Killigain shares the Casside reticence, both being active pursuers of the women who interest them, but several of the male heroes require the initiation of the more aggressive female. (Those who combine lecherous desire with a fear of what the neighbors will say, or sublimate sexual interest in puritanical sadism, are the special target of O'Casey's acid characterizations: minor characters in *The Star Turns Red*, *Cock-a-Doodle Dandy*, *The Bishop's Bonfire*, *The Drums of Father Ned*, and *Behind the Green Curtains*, as well as the main characters of the one-act "Bedtime Story" and the short story "I Wanna Woman," display these aspects and fare far worse at the hands of clever women than did the Covey tonguelashed by Rosie Redmond.) O'Casey seems to admire equally the self-assured lover and the shy lover. His finest depiction of the latter is the mysterious Messenger of *Cock-a-Doodle Dandy*, although only a minor character in a play dominated by women, and one whose primary role is a commentative voice, an auctorial spokesman. As the Messenger he arrives at the Marthraun house to deliver a telegram, but stays on to prophesy the doom of those who oppose the life-force of the supernatural Cock. As a flesh-and-blood character Robin is a young man in love with Marthraun's maid Marion, and has actually

been quite lively in his affair with her: he even spent
a month in jail for kissing her in public. He sings his
song to her ("Oh, woman gracious, in golden garments") and plies her with kisses despite the danger
of jail ("I'd do a year an' a day in a cold cell of pressed-in
loneliness, an' come out singin' a song, for a kiss from
a lass like Marion!"), but at the end of the play it is
Marion who takes the necessary initiative. Marthraun,
like Reiligan a Councillor and landowner, having become convinced that the forces of evil are operative
in his house because of his daughter Loreleen, recently
returned from perfidious England, banishes her with
the parish priest's blessing; his second wife, young
Lorna, decides to abandon Marthraun and go with
Loreleen, as does Marion. Robin has been watching
these events unfold and commenting acidly on Marthraun's attitudes, but he tries to hold Marion back with
kisses. "But not here, Robin Adair, oh, not here," she
insists; "for a whisper of love in this place bites away
some of th' soul! . . . Come, if you want to, Robin Adair;
stay, if you will." The Messenger also elects exile, following Marion out of Nyadnanave.

All of these masculine heroes in the O'Casey canon
carry with them aspects of the playwright himself, facets
of his personality, attitudes, ideas, and endorsements.
It remained, however, for the beginning of his autobiographical sketches evolving into the cumulative six
volumes to project an actual self-portrait in the young
Johnny Casside who becomes the playwright Sean Casside. Yet as he was finishing *Pictures in the Hallway*
and working on *Drums under the Window*, O'Casey

was simultaneously fashioning an expansion of the young Casside into the martyr hero of a workers' strike in *Red Roses for Me.* His Ayamonn Breydon is a tenement-dweller, a railroad worker, a young man living alone with his widowed mother. His interests are artistically eclectic: he acts, he draws, he writes, and he reads avidly (time permitting). "Sketchin', readin', makin' songs, an' learnin' Shakespeare," his mother complains, "if you had a piano, you'd be thryin' to learn music. Why don't you stick at one thing, an' leave the others alone?" In his romantic zeal Ayamonn has endowed his Catholic girl Sheila with overwhelming attributes, assuming that she would gladly share poverty with him while sharing his dreams: "A sober black shawl on her shoulders, a simple petticoat, and naked feet would fail to find her craving finer things that envious women love." The naive Ayamonn is equally fanciful about the danger of a railroad strike; although he is assisting in the organization of a fundraising show for the Union, he assumes that "there'll be no strike. The bosses won't fight. They'll grant the extra shilling a week demanded." Ayamonn is rather unpromising material for a potential hero. At best he might duplicate Johnny Casside's feat of knocking a policeman from his horse with a fallen lance once he is backed against the wall and can no longer run (earning him Daisy Battles's solicitous admiration).

The actual appearance of Sheila Moorneen at the Breydons' flat soon reveals Ayamonn's naiveté: she is as lovely as he insists, but she is far from brave and dreadfully bourgeois. She is close to buckling under parental disapproval of her association with a Protestant, and her only hope is that Ayamonn will abandon the workers' cause, sell out to the bosses, and earn himself a foreman's position. "Go to hell, girl, I have a soul to save as well as you," is Ayamonn's angry retort to Sheila. The strike has of course materialized as a reality, the demands for a shilling contemptuously rejected, and Ayamonn drops his playacting and songs for the ensuing conflict; both Sheila and his worried mother oppose his participation, but the Protestant minister, Mr. Clinton, who has come to warn Ayamonn of the employers' intentions of unleashing the police, refuses to forbid Ayamonn's involvement ("Who am I to say that God's against it? . . . If they be his brothers, he does well among them"), as a delegation of railwaymen ask Ayamonn to be one of their leaders. The dreamy Ayamonn shakes off his naiveté rather quickly now, as his sharp retort to Sheila shows, and begins to move like a tiger in action: "Tell the Committee, Bill, I'll be there; and that they honour me when they set me in front of my brothers. The Minstrel Show must be forgotten." Yet the third act of *Red Roses* begins to separate the central character from the realistic action of the play. Ayamonn is at first absent from O'Casey's depiction of Dublin slum streets along the river bank, and the human dregs that inhabit them. The minister and the police inspector, Ayamonn's protector and his adversary, walk together through the area, the clergyman revolted by the horrors of poverty and the policeman contemptuously superior to it all. Toward the end of the scene a crepuscular fantasy takes place, in which

Ayamonn dances in a poetic unreality with the tenement girl Finnoola, a radiant anticipation of the future that he is fighting for. "Dhreamin' I musta been," says the amazed Finnoola once the fantasy is over, "when I heard strange words in a city nearly smothered be stars, with God guidin' us along th' banks of a purple river, all of us clad in fresh garments, fit to make Osheen mad to sing a song of the revelry dancin' in an' out of God's own vision." O'Casey had experimented with this kind of expressionistic heightening of the drama in the war scene in *The Silver Tassie*, and utilized it again in *Red Roses* to broaden the scope and intensify the drama of the local situation. The city becomes the central focus of the play, the future its projected purpose.

The autobiographic Ayamonn has faded from the drama: the path bifurcates by which the actual O'Casey went on to become the playwright of his people depicted in *Inishfallen* and the exiled writer of *Rose and Crown* and *Sunset and Evening Star*, while the fictional Ayamonn leads the strike and is killed by the Inspector. His death takes place off-stage and is reported by the injured Finnoola: "He whispered it in me ear as his life fled through a bullet-hole in his chest—th' soldiers, th' soldiers. He said this day's but a day's work done, an' it'll be begun again tomorrow." He had entered the battle with his mother's blessing, having won her over to his cause, and now that he is dead even Sheila embraces his cause. When Inspector Finglas attempts to comfort her, hoping to replace the dead Ayamonn in her affections, she pushes him away with a curse.

She too has now understood the efficacy of Ayamonn's dream, commenting that "maybe he saw the shilling in th' shape of a new world." As such Sheila seems much closer to the dream he had had of her, the dream coming closest to perfecting his purpose in imaginative autobiography, in giving shape and voice and character to the most significant aspects of his lifelong ideals.

2
Casts of Characters

When Lady Gregory confided to O'Casey, during his Abbey Theatre days, that she considered characterization his strong point, her words must have been received with mixed reaction. O'Casey was in the habit of insisting that he could identify the prototype for each of his characters, and it should have been apparent that his efforts were very strongly in the direction of technique and approach in his dramas. But O'Casey's characters are destined to be remembered—particularly his unique comic creations—and no one more than his Paycock. The development of "Captain" Jack Boyle and his butty Joxer Daly in *Juno* is probably O'Casey's finest achievement. He continued thereafter to vary the possibilities of the character type, the indolent, self-indulgent braggart whom he saw at the crux of the paralytic condition in Irish life, but whose boisterous wit and élan always brought him at least halfway back to redemption. In dozens of varying situations O'Casey proved that variations on the type could be endless, and few of his plays were without them. The Captain's all-suffering wife Juno pinpoints his behavior as she conjectures that Boyle is "struttin' about the town like a paycock with Joxer, I suppose," and sums up his essence: "that's what he's waitin' for—till he thinks I'm gone to work, an' then sail in with the boul' Joxer, to burn all the coal an' dhrink all the tea in the place, to show them what a good Samaritan he is!" The soul of generosity on the product of Juno's earnings, Boyle buys the wavering loyalty of the parasitic Joxer when he can. He fulfills Juno's prophecy by treating his butty to tea and sausage—although he keeps the actual sausage for himself and gives Joxer only the drippings. When Jerry Devine comes with Father Farrell's message of a job, Boyle develops severe pains in his legs, and it is soon apparent that the paycock is displaying his full repertoire of tricks.

Boyle's predilection for playing the paycock is brought to its full height with the appearance of Bentham's news that Boyle is one of the heirs of a dead relative, and while the will is being probated the Boyles celebrate in style, buying generously on credit. This time-honored theatrical device allows the paycock more than enough rope with which to ensnare himself—he swears off the evil influence of Joxer Daly, leaving him out on the window ledge (where he had taken refuge when Juno arrived home unexpectedly and now hears news of the legacy) : "Juno, I'm done with Joxer; he's nothin' but a prognosticator an' a . . ." But Joxer does not stay out in the cold for long. Forgetting his fear of Juno, he emerges from his perch and denounces his betrayer, disclosing that he has always known about the Captain's deceptions: that he had never been to sea and that there was nothing wrong with his legs except laziness. Yet two days later the two butties are back together again, since the paycock is buying the drinks, and Joxer is fawning upon him as usual. The role of the Joxer figure is as comic foil; he is a lesser paycock, not quite able to bring off the greater audacities, and dependent upon the superior operator to include him in. Essentially he is alternately sycophantic and treacherous, at times crowing with admiration for Boyle's every act ("Ah, that's a darlin' song, a daaarlin' song!") and at others denouncing him as "Jacky Boyle, Esquire, infernal rogue an' damned liar!" Joxer's denunciation comes when he learns that the legacy has fallen through, that the will had been poorly worded and no money would ever be forthcoming (Charlie Bentham having disappeared), and Joxer has little to lose this time. Boyle tries to carry off the deception as long as he can, but the news spreads; the tailor reclaims the suit he made, and all the furniture is carried back to the store. The execution of Johnny, the discovery of Mary's pregnancy, and the end of the financial dream leave Juno a resolute woman, determined to start life again with her daughter. They abandon the empty flat, and when the paycock returns, drunk again and with Joxer in tow, it is to the desolation of a vacant apartment and his last sixpence, still unaware of Johnny's death and Juno's defection, but insisting that "th' whole worl's . . . in a terr . . . ible state o' . . . chassis!"

Several years later in *The Silver Tassie* O'Casey again

created a comic pair as relief from the seriousness of
Harry Heegan's pathetic drama. Heegan's father Sylvester is paired off with friend Simon Norton in the
now-familiar roles, but their importance is a good bit
diminished and their cowardice of far less significance.
Their supreme comic moments occur at four instances
in the play. In Act One they are being hounded by a
zealously evangelistic Susie Monican who sees them
as sinners ripe for salvation: "It's persecutin', that tam-
bourine theology of Susie's," Sylvester complains; "I
always get a curious, sickenin' feelin', Simon, when I
hear the Name of the Supreme Bein' tossed into the
quietness of a sensible conversation." Later in the same
act the two find themselves confronted by a violent
neighbor, Teddy Foran, who has run amok because of
his wife's infidelity; Sylvester at first is confident:
"Simon's a tidy little man with his fists, an' would make
Teddy Foran feel giddy if he got home with his left
hook"; but hearing the sound of a crash he soon modi-
fies his confidence: "I wonder is that Simon knockin'
down Foran, or Foran knockin' down Simon?" In Act
Three they are hospital patients in danger of being
ordered to bathe, Sylvester complaining, "Can't they
be content with an honest to God cleanliness, an' not
be tryin' to gild a man with soap and water." And in
Act Four they confront the new menace of a ringing
telephone: "I never handled a telephone in my life,"
says Sylvester; "I chanced it once and got so hot and
quivery that I couldn't hear a word, and didn't know
what I was saying myself," says Simon. In all they are a
tame pair of paycocks at best, having all the absurdity

of the breed but none of the real arrogance and vin-
dictiveness that marked Boyle and Daly. Against their
normal routine of bumbling ineffectiveness Harry lives
out his poignant drama, from the exultation of victory
to the despair of mutilation, Sylvester and Simon being
equally unable to cope with any of the facets of Harry
Heegan's fortunes. Instead they insulate themselves in
their self-contained world, hoping that all complexities
(Harry's paralysis and Harry's rage) will, like the ringing of the telephone, just stop.

Some of the one-act plays were written by O'Casey
as sketches for comic development to be used in varying
ways in larger works. In "A Pound on Demand," for
example, a couple of drunken workmen are seen in
their paycock-and-butty relationship to each other.
Sammy is the drunker of the two and attempting to
sign a postal order for a pound; Jerry is less drunk and
wily enough to realize that he stands to be treated on
the money. His efforts are painstakingly concentrated
on pulling Sammy together sufficiently so that the
signature could be effected and honored, and he must
hide his annoyance so as not to kill the golden goose. In
"The End of the Beginning" O'Casey introduces contrasting physical characteristics in his pair, Darry Berrill being stocky and bald, while Barry Derrill is thin
and mustachioed. The plot is an old one: wife and
husband exchange jobs for a while, she to mow the
meadow while he tends to the house. But complacent
Darry takes time out for exercising to music and is
joined by Barry, until they are involved in an intermin-
able quarrel. The actual job at hand goes no better.

Barry's near-sighted assistance supplements Darry's egregious inefficiency, and the place is a shambles by the time Mrs. Berrill gets back. In this case the paycock figure is again aggressive and pompous, attempting to bulldoze his way through, while the butty knows he is being put upon but is nonetheless intimidated.

In the later plays O'Casey elevates the social status of his paycock pair, but the personality traits remain very much the same. In *Cock-a-Doodle Dandy* Michael Marthraun is the owner of a "lucrative bog" (once having been only a small farmer) and Sailor Mahan is now the owner of a "fleet of lorries" transporting turf. They are in the process of arguing over the price of transporting Marthraun's turf when all the supernatural events take place in rapid succession in the Marthraun house. They quarrel over the price, each insisting that increased demands by his workers makes the increase impossible to pay (Marthraun) or impossible to concede (Mahan) ; moments of great friendship bring the negotiations full circle, only to have new animosities set the two against each other again. Mahan seems a good deal more likeable: he is less superstitious and more reasonable, refusing to believe Marthraun's wild conjectures that his daughter is evil, but by the end of the play he shows himself to be a self-seeking hypocrite, having attempted to buy Loreleen's favor with the money she needs to escape Nyadnanave. Sadistic vigilantes interrupt the seduction, and report that they "pelted him back to his home an' proper wife . . . an' he's there now, in bed, an' sorry for what he thried to do." Marthraun, having arrogantly banished Loreleen, finds himself suddenly aware of the possible loneliness that awaits him in his empty house, and when he asks, "What, Messenger, would you advise me to do?", Robin answers, "Die. There is little else left useful for the likes of you to do."

O'Casey's next play, *The Bishop's Bonfire*, portrayed an extension of Councillor Marthraun in Councillor Reiligan, "the biggest money-man in the district, a loyal pillar of the clergy," who "has a great power and influence in the affairs of the state." He has none of his predecessor's pathetic qualities, nor does he endear himself sufficiently to have a friend: the Canon is his only companion, but theirs is a political arrangement, hardly a friendship. Reiligan's son considers him a tightwad; his daughter Keelin hates him because he has frightened the boy she loves into complete submission in order to marry her to a rich old farmer; and his daughter Foorawn, given to the Church, is completely indifferent to him. Reiligan reigns as the local autocrat, his only redeeming touch being his accurate evaluation of Manus Moanroe's worth as a foreman. Actually, there is another "pair" in *The Bonfire* better qualified for the role of paycocks, the two masons, the Catholic Rankin and the Protestant Carranaun (known as the Prodical): self-righteousness, prudery, and argumentativeness are their essential characteristics, while a fear of the evil in liquor and women torments them, so that Manus sums them up in his comment to the Prodical: "I don't know which of you's the bigger bum—him who thinks he's given to heaven, or you who know you're given to drink." Their quarrels over a brick are the stuff that paycock-joxer friendships are made of. (Not only in "A Pound on Demand," but also in *Purple Dust*, O'Casey had previously shown pairs of proletarian paycocks; in the latter the first and third workmen have a grand time moving a quattrocento desk through a doorway and ruining it with their hob-nailed boots, to the tune of such advice as: "give it a sudden swing to the ayste, an' while she's swingin' we'll shoot her ahead.")

By the time the paycock character had run its course, in *The Drums of Father Ned*, he was reduced by O'Casey to thorough ineffectuality, despite his public elevation from Councillor to Mayor of Doonavale. Aloysius Binnington has come a long way. O'Casey describes him as a "business-man, patriot, and pietist" who "loves himself more than anything else living or dead, though he isn't really a bad chap." Along with him, in this, one of O'Casey's most benign comedies, has come his arch-enemy, Deputy-Mayor McGilligan. They have not spoken to each other in decades, but have been doing business together nonetheless; they married sisters, and their two children, Michael Binnington and Nora McGilligan, are spending a great deal of time together, much to the parents' chagrin. There is no time now to do anything about this situation, for the businessmen are secretly dealing in Russian timber, in cahoots with a businessman from Ulster. Their three-way disputes become legion, while all the young people in Doonavale, inspired by a mysteriously free-spirited Father Ned, are preparing a festive Tostal celebration, to the constant annoyance of the ineffec-

tual parish priest, Father Fillifogue. All of this comes
to a head with the discovery of the Communist timber
in Doonavale, but even more serious is the sudden
realization that the two politicians have forgotten to
file for re-election, that Michael and Nora have filed
to run for Mayor and Deputy-Mayor, and admit sleep-
ing together in college (with no palliative of a "registry
marriage" to take the bite out of their open defiance).
As the young people go off to the sound of Father Ned's
revolutionary drum, the businessmen and the priest
are left virtually atrophied. The Ulsterman tries to
rouse them, before he too joins the march to the drums:

> Wauk up! Are ye no' gangin' tae make a ficht o' it? If
> ye dinna, oor business'll be no comfort in th' future. Is
> it deid dunne ye all are, or what? I'd no' give in. [*He
> shakes Binnington.*] Awauk, mon, on' dinna lut your
> dondher dee! [*He shakes Father Fillifogue.*] Are ye no'
> gangin' tae ootface yon Feyther Nud?

Not all of the playwright's paycock types were Irish,
however, nor were they all males. An odd pair of pay-
hens is presented in the opening scene of *Behind the
Green Curtains*, where hoydens Lizzie and Angela, having forsworn drink forever, have a comic dispute over
a poster of Charles Stewart Parnell, attempting to decide
whether it is St. Peter or St. Joseph. Having agreed to
take a small drop, they return at the end of the scene
in the deplorable condition made famous by Boyle and
Daly, and duplicated by Sammy and Jerry. ("For Jasus'
sake Angela," beseeches the drunken Lizzie, "thry to
pull yourself together.") In *Purple Dust* the two British
landlords reveal close affinities to such socially disparate

paycocks as Boyle and his butty, as they attempt to lord
it over each other as well as over their employees. The
natural physical, intellectual, and spiritual superiority
of O'Killigain and O'Dempsey reduces Stoke and Poges
to an atrophy much like that which ensnares Binnington, McGilligan, and Father Fillifogue. (O'Casey's
lower-class paycocks have a personal charm and élan
missing in autocratic versions of the species, whether
upper-class English or parvenu Irish.) In all fairness
to the bumbling Britishers it should be noted that
O'Casey himself felt no particular malice toward them,
but commented in a later essay that they are "foolish,
inept, pompous; but they are comic, at times pathetic,
and all through likeable. But Time and Change do not
care a damn for these lovable things, neither can the
playwright care either. All that they are, and all they
represent, must go."

Poges and Stoke bound onto the stage with mistresses
and servants singing delightedly of the "bosky countrie,"
but soon find the irritating discrepancy between the
facts and their fancies: bird noises keep them awake at
night and the cold morning finds them uncomfortable
and miserable; a mismanaged lawnroller crashes
through the house, knocking down a wall; Basil Stoke
is thrown by his wild Irish horse, and Avril nimbly
rides off with O'Killigain instead; Basil has his revenge
against the Irish animal kingdom by shooting a wild
bull in the house, but it turns out to be only a harmless
cow brought over for sale; a yellow bearded workman
keeps making haphazard holes in the ceiling for electric
outlets; telephone connections to the London brokers

prove difficult because the local operator refuses to put through calls at night; and the quattrocento desk fares badly at the hands of the casual workmen. Ireland and the Irish, the past and the present, all seem to conspire against the landlords, who cannot bring themselves to admit that they have no real appetite for roughing it in the country, nor any aptitude for it. Their Irish mistresses in particular prove difficult to handle, since the men have unwittingly made them financially independent by settling a tidy sum on each. Poges and Stoke attempt to scoff at the opposition, underestimating the inherent superiority of O'Killigain and O'Dempsey. And in the end the predicted Flood comes, and they are left pathetically stranded.

Even in their behavior to each other, Cyril Poges and Basil Stoke betray their concept of comradeship as no better than that of Boyle and Daly. (Their tagnames, incidentally, are fine O'Casey touches: Stoke Poges is the setting of Gray's "Elegy Written in a Country Churchyard," so that *Purple Dust* serves as a parody of that idyllic vision of rural life; and Cyril and Basil derive from the Greek for lordly and kingly respectively.) Poges is a self-made man who resents Stoke's cockiness about being an Oxford graduate, and intellectual discussions between the two are little better than Boyle's lectures to Joxer. Basil's disputation on the primrose—"Try to think, sir, of a primrose, not as a primrose, but as a simple object, and as a substance outside of yourself"—meets with a hardheaded rebuttal from the blunt Poges, bringing Stoke close to tears. Souhaun sardonically reminds Poges that his com-

panion "passed through Oxford," but Poges only re-
torts: "I don't care if he crept under it or flew over it;
he's not going to punish me with what he picked up
there." Poges's is the pigheaded pride of the man who
made his own money and can now command respect
from those beneath him. He makes even worse gaffes
with O'Killigain and O'Dempsey, assuming that these
crude folk would instinctively respect his position, and
therefore corroborate his ideas, but both are equally
outspoken in asserting their greater knowledge. When
he carelessly calls O'Dempsey a fool, Poges receives a
learned disquisition on the history of Irish culture
which leaves him stunned. "Cheeking me up to my
very face!", he complains to Souhaun. He assumes that
O'Killigain will respect the sanctity of the lord-vassal
relationship between them, and is equally nonplussed
by the vassal's insolent manner. Still expecting acquiescence from him, Poges delivers a eulogy on the greatness of England, but O'Killigain remains unimpressed:

> Poges [loudly]. I say, sir, that Justice is England's old
> nurse; Righteousness and Peace sit together in her
> common-room, and the porter at her gate is Truth!
> O'Killigain [quietly, but sarcastically]. An' God Himself
> is England's butler.

Compared to O'Killigain and O'Dempsey the Oxford-
educated Basil is better fare for the intellectual style
of Cyril Poges, who sounds no better than Captain
Boyle when he tries to remember "one of the chief gods
of the ancient Celts," rejecting such suggestions as Gog
or Magog, and Gulliver, but contenting himself with
the decision that his name was Brobdingnag.

O'Casey throughout his career allowed himself a

broad range of play in handling the paycock as a type, often stressing the individuality of the character at the expense of known characteristics, and finding some more redeemable than others. That they strut with a measure of self-importance, that they fabricate outrageously to preserve their self-esteem, and that they often see others around them as reflections of themselves serve to establish the type. How they react when the chips are down often distinguished the individual. Seumas Shields apparently displays elements of the species in his superstitions and cowardice, his contempt for Minnie Powell, and his attributing to Maguire the laziness which is actually his own. Yet Seumas is well-read and far more adroit in his understanding of the purpose of literature than Donal, and at times O'Casey delights in making him the source of some unexpected jabs: "That's the Irish People all over," he says in irritation, "they treat a joke as a serious thing and a serious thing as a joke. Upon me soul, I'm beginning to believe that the Irish people aren't, never were, an' never will be fit for self-government." Seumas is of course condemning himself unwittingly along with the rest of the Irish People (as Donal is quick to remind him when he makes a sardonic joke of Maguire's death), but the degree to which O'Casey allows the statement to stand as a possible truth verifies Shields's perceptiveness about others. He is at his best when he deplores the senseless killings and the misdirected efforts of the Republican gunmen:

> It's the civilians that suffer; when there's an ambush they don't know where to run. Shot in the back to save the British Empire, an' shot in the breast to save the soul of Ireland. I'm a Nationalist meself, right enough—a

Nationalist right enough, but all the same—I'm a Nationalist right enough; I believe in the freedom of Ireland, an' that England has no right to be here, but I draw the line when I hear the gunmen blowin' about dyin' for the people, when it's the people that are dyin' for the gunmen! With all due respect to the gunmen, I don't want them to die for me.

O'Casey's technique of interlacing such accuracies with inane bits and pieces like the tapping on the wall assures him of a rounded comic character, and in Fluther Good (*The Plough and the Stars*) and Feelim O'Morrigun (*Oak Leaves and Lavender*) he extended the individual potentials of the type established with Seumas.

Feelim occupies a unique position as the rare Irishman in an otherwise British setting, having misrepresented himself sufficiently to obtain a position as a butler in the Hatherleigh household. Without references or previous experience Feelim nonetheless distinguishes himself by his hard work and uncommon efficiency. (O'Casey is of course reversing the stereotypic image of the stage-Irishman.) As the German bombs fall around him, Feelim refuses either to return to neutral Ireland or to lose heart, but emerges as that rare individual who rises above his environment and circumvents unusual hardships. During the first act in particular Feelim reveals those paycock traits that count against him, but he continues to develop throughout the drama into one of O'Casey's unusually fine people —though hardly ever perfect. It is obvious from the first that Feelim is short-tempered and impatient with the shortcomings of others: he calls Mary a fool for "putting a blackout up in th' dark, an' steppin' from th' window-sill on to a chair that wasn't there," and Tom another fool for not being "able to drive a nail into wood without shoving his hand through a window and cutting a vein open!" He also betrays a puritanical touch, disapproving of a bawdy song (which turns out to be Shakespeare), although he has already declared that he has no use for the puritan-minded: "Odd man, your old man," he comments to Monica; "His conscience is a menace to most people. I never could understand men interested in religion." In paycock fashion Feelim has no qualms about condemning in others characteristics which are apparent in himself. When Monica explains about the ghosts that presumably haunt the Hatherleigh mansion, Feelim frantically crosses himself ("Jesus, Mary an' Joseph between us an' all harm!"). Although temperamentally mercurial he is also capable of a solidly stable reaction to difficulties, and his sympathetic and delicate handling of the pathetically dotty Dame Hatherleigh remains constant throughout the play.

Feelim's position in *Oak Leaves* is ostensibly that of a bystander, a central figure around whom most of the action takes place. Drishogue has enlisted in the Royal Air Force and is eager for battle against the Nazis; he is in love with Monica Penrhyn, who looks upon Feelim as her real father, since the violent pacifist, Abraham Penrhyn, strongly disapproves of her alliance with a combatant. Drishogue is killed in combat, as are Dame Hatherleigh's husband, and son, and it is Feelim who remains the Dame's supporting strength. But with

Drishogue gone, *Oak Leaves and Lavender* is left without the author's spokesman, the voice that had ex-
plained the necessity of victory over fascism and defended the Soviet Union against the red-baiting of Mrs.
Tutting. Feelim, however, moves into Drishogue's
shoes: he had already attacked the cowardly pacifism
of Pobjoy by asserting that "thousands of children
who never took the sword perished by it . . . because we took it into our hands a little late"; and he
attacked de Valera and the new theocracy in Eire,
"turnin' the poor people into shock brigades of con-
fraternities an' holy sight-seein' sodalities, so that they're
numb with kneelin', an' hoarse with th' dint of recitin'
litany an' prayer!" Now he declares himself his son's
successor: "Here on this spot, at this moment, Feelim
O'Morrigun takes up th' fight where Drishogue laid it
down!" O'Casey has chosen his Irish hero not only from
the political elite, the young Communist idealists, but
also from the very ordinary run of humanity, the source
material that usually provides vain and useless paycocks. But Feelim is never to become the ideal figure
that Drishogue had been. He remains fallible and human throughout, so that although he declares Drishogue's fight to be his own now, he is still unable to
transcend his moralistic background: he remains
shocked that Monica and Drishogue have only had a
registry marriage, insisting that "the gettin' o' children
should be done accordin' to rule!"

In many ways it is Fluther Good that is O'Casey's
most important creation and his finest comic character
(the name alone is a gem, since "to be fluthered" is

Dublin argot for being drunk). Fluther emerges from *The Plough* as a dominant personage, and he goes on to have an individual existence for his creator outside of the play itself: at various times in the autobiographies O'Casey speculates what Fluther Good would have done in a particular situation. He pits the drunken Fluther against Yeats in a Merrion Square salon, for example. Not that Fluther was an embodiment of all the virtues (Drishogue and Red Jim and O'Killigain would serve better as such), but that he is decidedly more human, a welcome companion despite his faults. There is much in the man that would disqualify him as an O'Casey "hero"—those paycock traits are easily detectable. His religion is both conventional and hypo-critical, as on one hand he champions Adam and Eve against the Covey's insistence on "mollycewels an' atoms," while on the other he announces that "Fluther has a vice versa opinion of them that put ivy leaves into their prayer-books, scabbin' it on th' clergy, an' thryin' to out-do th' haloes o' th' saints be lookin' as if he was wearin' around his head a glittherin' aroree boree allis!" Also, Fluther shares with many another O'Caseyan Dubliner a rather rigid attitude toward the physical, absurdly assuming that a Giorgione painting of Venus is a photograph of a naked model and con-demning it as a terrible and shocking picture. (It is to his credit, however, that he gallantly rescues Rosie Redmond from the Covey's abuse, and lets himself be led home by her.)

Like Feelim he too is essentially a witness to the action, to the tragic events that befall the others. Central to the tragedy are such characters as Nora Clitheroe and her husband Jack. Prior to the Rising Jack had divorced himself from the Citizen Army, offended that he was not given a commission, and Nora jealously clings to him for fear that he will be lured away by the glamor of the uniform. The commission as Commandant had in fact been made, but Nora kept the news from him, and now Jack shakes her off and reports to his unit. During the fighting the frantic wife goes in search of her husband, and it is Fluther who goes to the barricades to bring her back. When Mollser Gogan dies of consumption in the midst of the fighting, it is again Fluther who does what has to be done. "I'll never forget what you done for me, Fluther," Mrs. Gogan says, "goin' around at th' risk of your life settlin' every-thing with th' undhertaker an' th' cemetery people. When all me own were afraid to put their noses out, you plunged like a good one through hummin' bullets, an' they knockin' fire out o' th' road, tinklin' through th' frightened windows, an' splashin' themselves to pieces on th' walls!" Fluther's quiet heroism is as much a part of him as his drinking and looting: during the action he liberated a half-gallon of whiskey. In the last act Fluther and Peter and the Covey play cards with Capt. Brennan (now in civilian clothes) when the British soldiers enter the tenement, and the four men are led away to confinement (as O'Casey himself had been).

Yet Fluther's heroism in *The Plough and the Stars* is of secondary importance to that of a woman, Bessie Burgess. The 45-year-old carpenter is a sufficiently un-likely source in searching for a hero, but the loud-

mouthed, drunken fruit-vendor is even more unpromising. O'Casey, who was particularly interested in the
woman as a potential for courage, manages to reverse
a multitude of unfortunate impressions in order to
salvage Bessie for heroism. His technique is to shock
the audience with Bessie's offensiveness, maintain elements of the offending traits, introduce redeeming
features halfway through, and develop those features
until they dominate the situation. This assures both
consistency of character development and a surprising
but logical change. The initial impression derives from
Bessie's abuse of Nora, whom she drunkenly assails for
bourgeois pretensions ("You little over-dressed throl-
lope, you, for one pin I'd paste th' white face o' you!")
—it requires Fluther to restrain her and Jack to eject
her. As a Protestant loyalist with a son in the British
Army, Bessie is the bane of her Catholic neighbors, and
in the pub scene, while the patriots are being stirred by
revolutionary fervor, Bessie harangues Mrs. Gogan with
taunts about "poor little Catholic Belgium." Mrs.
Gogan and Bessie Burgess square off as natural antag-
onists, the Catholic shrew and the Protestant shrew
abusing each other with a barrage of personal invective,
until both are thrown out of the pub, Mrs. Gogan
leaving her infant behind. There is very little choice
between the two women up to this point, although Mrs.
Gogan's act of maternal carelessness might put her at
a disadvantage with a humane audience.

It is in the third act that Bessie begins to evolve
as something other than a disreputable harridan. At
first she is seen shouting her usual invective from

her window: the Rising has begun, and she excoriates
those who are "stabbin' in th' back th' men that are
dyin' in th' threnches for them!" But the looting
manages to level natural antagonisms, and when
squabbling for an abandoned pram produces a stale-
mate, Bessie and Jinny Gogan pool their resources
and decide to share the vehicle, going off together to
collect their loot. Small acts of kindness to the con-
sumptive Mollser have already been performed sur-
reptitiously by Bessie, preparing us for the larger
gesture at the end of the act—Nora is in desperate
need of a doctor. She had attempted to restrain Jack
from returning to the battle, but he had cast her off
and gone, and the pregnant Nora has begun to
hemorrhage. Fluther is too drunk and Mrs. Gogan does
not dare leave Mollser, so the responsibility is left
to Bessie: "I'll risk it . . . Give her a little of Fluther's
whisky. . . . Go on back to her, you," she says to Mrs.
Gogan, and she prays as she goes out, "Oh God, be
Thou my help in time o' throuble. An' shelter me
safely in th' shadow of Thy wings!"

The full emergence of heroic Bessie Burgess comes
in the final act. The scene is in Bessie's attic flat, where
the wildly distracted Nora is being cared for by Bessie.
The baby, born dead, is in a coffin with dead Mollser,
awaiting burial, and Nora's condition is reported by
the Covey:

> Th' docthor thinks she'll never be th' same; thinks she'll
> be a little touched here. [*He touches his forehead.*] She's
> ramblin' a lot; thinkin' she's out in th' counthry with
> Jack; or gettin' his dinner ready for him before he
> comes home; or yellin' for her kiddie. All that, though,

might be th' chloroform she got. . . . I don't know what
we'd have done only for oul' Bessie: up with her for
th' past three nights, hand runnin'.

Captain Brennan arrives with the news of Jack Clitheroe's death, but Nora is far too distracted to understand, and calls for her husband and her baby. In her
delirium she rushes to the window, and Bessie, attempting to pry her away and return her to bed, is
shot by a sniper. She curses Nora (as she had done in
the first scene), "I've got this through . . . through
you . . . through you, you bitch, you!" But her dying
words are: "Jesus Christ, me sight's goin'! It's all dark,
dark! Nora, hold me hand!" Bessie's death seems to jar
Nora from her delirium, and as she is led away by Mrs.
Gogan to "doss in poor Mollser's bed," there is the
horrible possibility that Nora has yet to face the full
realization of all that has happened. Even Jinny Gogan,
in her final gesture as Bessie's replacement, shows signs
of the kind of redemption that Bessie proved capable
of. The apotheosis of Bessie Burgess had been carefully
prepared by the playwright, from kindness to Mollser
to self-sacrifice for Nora, all the while continuing to
sing her hymns in defiance of her neighbors, taunt the
Irish and uphold her loyalty to the Crown. And during
the last scene she mentions to the British soldiers what
she has hitherto told no one: that her son has been
wounded in action in France and is being returned
home.

If O'Casey's treatment of Bessie is surprising, it is
not an isolated surprise: his attitude toward women
as stronger individuals remained consistent throughout

his career. The pathetic weaknesses of Seumas and Donal made Minnie Powell look strong by comparison, but although only an ignorant tenement girl she proved to be magnificent. Her faults were common enough— and Seumas was quick to uncover them: "an ignorant little bitch that thinks of nothin' but jazz dances, fox-trots, picture theatres an' dress." (Nora Clitheroe and Sheila Moorneen are similar in limitations.) Her infatuation with Donal is enough to transform her into a selfless heroine. She had assumed that the bravery was his, and admits to him her girlish trepidations: *"I'm* all of a tremble when I hear a shot go off, an' what must it be in the middle of the firin'?" Yet her real bravery is already ingrained in a very different form, but one which determines the basic condition. Seumas is worried about what the "oul' ones" in the tenement will gossip when it becomes known that Minnie visits Donal in his flat, and even Donal expresses this concern to her. But Minnie is adamant: "An' do you think Minnie Powell cares whether they'll talk or no? She's had to push her way through life up to this without help from any one, an' she's not goin' to ask their leave, now, to do what she wants to do." O'Casey often distinguishes between the uselessly spineless and the potentially courageous by having his people commit themselves on their regard or disdain for what the neighbors will say.

The most admired woman in the O'Casey plays is Juno Boyle, a nagging wife who blooms into mature heroism under adverse circumstances. In many ways she is an inauspicious character in the first scene. She is often prosaically conventional in her thinking, since she cannot see why Mary should be on strike in support of a fired fellow-worker or why Johnny should risk losing an arm for a political principle. While the Captain is often a charming figure of fun, Juno is drab and humorless, as well as self-righteous, and somewhat ludicrous in blaming Boyle's condition on the bugaboo of evil companionship: "There'll never be any good got o' him so long as he goes with that shouldher-shruggin' Joxer. I killin' meself workin', an he sthruttin' about from mornin' till night like a paycock!" And Juno welcomes the announced windfall with typically bourgeois expectations, kowtowing to Charlie Bentham and joining in the preening before the neighbors. But when the full brunt of the series of tragedies falls, it is only Juno who is capable of holding the pieces together. She realizes when Johnny dies that she had been only superficially sympathetic with Mrs. Tancred, offering her a chair and a cup of tea. Boyle pretends that nothing has happened when it is apparent that the dream of wealth has disintegrated, and he curses his daughter when he learns of her pregnancy. But Juno marshals her resources, cuts herself free from the useless Captain and the empty apartment, and goes off with Mary to start a new life, one that she knows full well will always be a hard one. Grief, self-awareness, and determination are all present in her attitude now, as on one hand she says, "Maybe I didn't feel sorry enough for Mrs. Tancred when her poor son was found as Johnny's been found now," while on the other she decides on a plan of action:

> We'll go. Come, Mary, an' we'll never come back here agen. Let your father furrage for himself now; I've done

all I could an' it was all no use—he'll be hopeless till the end of his days. I've got a little room in me sisther's where we'll stop till your throuble is over, an' then we'll work together for the sake of the baby.

Many of O'Casey's young girls lack Mrs. Boyle's pervading strength. Mary Boyle from the first is torn between two opposing forces within her, as the author notes in his description of her: "one, through the circumstances of her life, pulling her back; the other, through the influence of books she has read, pushing her forward." In the last scene Mary has all but surrendered to the "circumstances of her life": she blames God for her condition, bemoans the fact that her child will be fatherless, and is terrified at the idea that she may have to go to see the dead body of her brother. It is only Juno's strength and sense that rescue her. Minnie Powell, who has read no books, stands up far better to her life. In effect, Minnie and Mary generate two different strains of young women, and it is not a penchant for pretty dresses that differentiates them. (Both Mary and Minnie are interested in dress, and O'Casey is consistent in preferring girls who want to look attractive.) Those who can say yes to life, as Minnie can, despite the "circumstances," are his natural heroines, but he is sympathetic with those young women who cannot, who fall apart like Nora Clitheroe or are rescued only by dint of a strong-willed mother. In *The Bishop's Bonfire* O'Casey presents two beleaguered sisters, Foorawn and Keelin Reiligan, and carefully traces the differences in their reactions to their environment.

Foorawn and Keelin are swept up in the preparations

for the anticipated visit to Ballyoonagh of the bishop, a native son whose return is to be celebrated with a giant bonfire of books and pictures. Councillor Reiligan and Canon Burren are directing the preparations, and expect to profit from the visit by strengthening the hold of the Church on the morals of the townspeople. Foorawn's special position as a devout relieves her of the menial duties of the household, but all other members of the family and staff are feverishly involved, although some (like Manus and the Codger) are openly contemptuous of the proceedings, and the gentle Father Boheroe definitely suspicious of the outcome. Foorawn has in effect turned her back on life and on Manus, but Keelin suspects that Foorawn has not been altogether successful in denouncing the outside world: "If I know anything, there's silk knickers an' nylon stockin's under the skirt that feels so sober an' looks so black." But Foorawn insists that clothed in somber blue and black she is no longer alluring to Manus, and her icy demeanor with him and her condemnation of him as a spoiled priest persist until her death-wound, when all that she kept frozen and remote breaks through to acknowledge her dying love. Keelin, however, has pretended no such state of pious chastity and is openly in love with Dan Clooncoohy, a workman assisting the masons building a wall in the Reiligan garden. It is apparent that Councillor Reiligan will never consent to Keelin marrying a common laborer. (If one daughter has been given to the Church, the other is scheduled for a rich old farmer.) But Keelin and Dan insist upon their love for each other and receive Father Boheroe's blessing. The Councillor intercedes immediately, and the brave Dan capitulates completely: he is contrite before Reiligan and the Canon, but the next day decides to leave Ballyoonagh and abandon Keelin. "I was ready to defy them all," Keelin asserts, but Dan does not have the courage necessary to stay and fight or take Keelin with him. The Councillor and the Canon proceed with their plans to marry Keelin to Farmer Mullarkey, the Bishop's brother (against the objections of both). Nonetheless, Keelin remains obdurate, though the best she can do is organize a kitchen rebellion against preparing the feast for the bishop. And when the others surrender to the cajoling of the Canon, only Keelin holds out in defiance: "I hope yous'll all be settled spiced in hell, soon, the whole of yous hungry; with flocks of plucked plovers yous can't catch flyin' round yous!"

Foorawn's defeat is bitter, and Keelin's victory only a pyrrhic one. Other O'Casey heroines fare a good deal better, especially in the happier comedies. Nora McGilligan and the servant girl Bernadette Shillayley in *The Drums of Father Ned* succeed from the very beginning in dancing rings around the fossilized symbols of local authority, Bernadette merrily playing the Binnington piano despite snobbish restrictions from the Mayor and his wife, and Nora happily having her affair with Michael Binnington. "Well, we studied at the same College," Nora begins; "An' we lived in the same flat," Michael adds; "An' slept in th' same bed o' Sundays," Nora concludes. Bernadette is not particularly shy in her lovemaking either; when Tom Killsallighan is rather reticent as a lover, she takes the initiative, and quoting Father Ned as gospel, has no difficulty in convincing him to be a bit bolder. In all the spirit of the Tostal and the drum of the puckish cleric combine to arouse the young people of Doonavale, and they take command over the fossilized remains of parents and parish priest.

Victory is not as easy in *Cock-a-Doodle Dandy*, where except for the support of the Messenger, the three women have to fight the battle against inordinate odds. The spirit of the Cock attempts to offset the prevailing gloom of the atrophied town of Nyadnanave, but Father Domineer, One-eyed Larry, and old Shanaar conspire to exorcise the Marthraun house of the free and jubilant spirit. When Loreleen is driven from the community, her stepmother hurries to join her: "I go with you love, I've got a sthrong pair of shoes in the sack you can put on when we're free from th' Priest an' his rabble. Lift up your heart, lass: we go not towards an evil, but leave an evil behind us!" Unable to win out against Marthraun and Father Domineer, the young women choose exile instead. As does Reena Kilternan in *Behind the Green Curtains*: the exodus from Ballybeedhust begins when Noneen Melbayle, Chatastray's housekeeper, is attacked by Catholic vigilantes who do not approve of a young girl working for an unmarried man (despite her father's approval). Chatastray is of course ineffectual in protecting her. So Boeman is taking her to England where "she'll stop with me married sister an' me till she settles into a job, an' afther, if she wants to." When Chatastray disappoints Reena as well, she too joins Boeman and Noneen for England, the last of a long parade of O'Casey characters to follow him into exile.

For Reena the events that befall her because she insists upon entering the Protestant church to pay her respects to a dead patron of letters result in a political education, as the strike and Ayamonn's death proved to be for Sheila, but other O'Casey heroines know what they want from the beginning. A girl like Julia in *The Star Turns Red* is already politically as well as amorously allied with her Communist lover, but even she at first balks at having to attend a union meeting when she is eager to go dancing. She soon learns her mistake, and thereafter remains resolute with clenched fist throughout, the deaths of her father and of Jack reinforcing her political determination. Monica Penrhyn in *Oak Leaves and Lavender* is even devoid of that moment of hesitation: Drishogue's beliefs are hers and she subscribes to them, adding a determination of her own to have Drishogue's child. "I wanted a pledge of all he meant to me; and I got it; and I'm glad." Her counterpart in the play, Jennie, in love with Drishogue's friend Edgar Hatherleigh, is also a high-spirited and lively woman, but when Edgar's plane is shot down, Jennie rushes into the burning wreck and dies with him. One report suggests that she purposely chose to die with her lover, while another indicates that she died in an attempt to rescue him. In either case O'Casey makes no comment: it is apparent that he enthusiastically approves of Jennie and has no cause to try to judge her. But it is also apparent that he prefers Monica's plan of attack, her belief in life and Drishogue's ideals, and her intention to carry on with the engendering of new life amidst all the killing.

It is this avowal of life that is fundamental with the young heroines that O'Casey admires, and Avril and Souhaun have a good measure of it. The purple dust that is in danger of being blown away or inundated by the Flood emanates from the dead past, and the two lovely women are soon enlisted by the Irish heroes to escape from the impending disaster. Both have allied themselves with the rich Englishmen for the financial security offered, but have too much vitality to endure the dead life for long. At 33 Souhaun is not so confident as the younger Avril, but O'Killigain's flattery and O'Dempsey's sincere proposal overcome her reluctance, and as she listens to Philib she decides that "it's right an' lovely listenin' to a voice that's makin' gold embroidery out o' dancin' words." There is little doubt that O'Casey is unconcerned with any moral censure of the behavior of the two women, and Avril has no intention—now that she is going off with Jack—of giving up the jewels that Basil had bestowed on her: "I gave more than I got, you gilded monkey. It's winnowed of every touch of life I'd be if I stayed with th' waste of your mind much longer. . . . Th' thrinkets I wormed out of you are all here, an' here they stay, for th' wages were low for what was done for you."

O'Casey rarely makes moral condemnations of any sort, and even professional prostitutes appear in his plays as his avowed heroines. It is clear, however, that

O'Casey shows no particular approval of Jessie Taite in *The Silver Tassie*; her adoration of Harry in the first act proves merely opportunistic—he is the hero of the moment and she basks in his reflected glory. Harry's pal, Barney Bagnal, is reduced to sycophantic hero worship, and even the drably pious Susie Monican dotes on Harry Heegan, rebuffing Barney's attempt at familiarity. When the fortunes of war return Harry as a cripple and Barney as the hero who saved his life, Jessie makes the easy transition from past to present, ignoring the ruined Harry who now disgusts her and choosing the new victor. Susie too has undergone a transformation, having given up her pious vocation to become a nurse and her enforced frigidity to become Surgeon Maxwell's mistress. Susie is now vibrant with life, reborn as a beautiful and animated woman. Sylvester Norton comments that Susie is now "fashion'd like a Queen of Sheba," adding: "God moves in a mysterious way, Simon." Susie herself is quite specific about the change in her view of life: "After the sober rain of yesterday," she notes, "it is good to feel the new grace of the yellowing trees, and to get the fresh smell of the grass."

Three of O'Casey's heroines are even closer to the professional type, but to differing degrees and with different results: Jannice, the Young Woman of *Within the Gates* (originally listed as the Young Whore in the first printed edition, but changed thereafter), Rosie Redmond in *The Plough* (who engendered rioting in the Abbey Theatre), and the delightful Angela Nightingale in the short "Bedtime Story." Jannice is one of the author's most tragic heroines. Although lovely and full of life she is beset with fears; penniless she attempts to sell herself whenever possible, but O'Casey comments that "she is deficient in self-assurance, and is too generous and sensitive to be a clever whore, and her heart is not in the business." Her drunken mother abuses her whenever she can find Jannice, and she is prey to the men who frequent the park (at the end of the first scene she is arrested by a policewoman for soliciting): she hopes that the Gardener will marry her, but his interest in her is selfish and temporary; she pleads with her stepfather to take her back, but he has set up a home for her on several occasions, only to have her walk out. The Dreamer is interested in Jannice, but when he has no money she can ill afford the luxury of loyalty to him, and she goes off with the Salvation Army Officer instead. Soon she is back in Hyde Park, and the Bishop begins to take an ambivalent interest in her, beginning to suspect that he is actually her father, the theology student who had abandoned her mother when she was pregnant. The money that the Bishop gives the Dreamer for Jannice he uses to buy Jannice's favors, but his songs do succeed in winning her to him. Yet her fears of the torments of hell conjured up by the nuns remain pervasive, for Jannice realizes that her heart is bad and that she might die at any time. The Bishop tries to convince her to repent, while the Dreamer tries to convince her to live life to the fullest, shouting fiercely, "Sing them silent, dance them still, laugh them into an open shame!"— but while she dances wildly and shouts, "I'll go the last few steps of the way rejoicing; I'll go, go game, and I'll die dancing!", her death is somewhat ambiguous. To the Bishop's delight she makes the sign of the cross with her last effort, but the Dreamer nonetheless rejoices in her bravery: "You fought the good fight, Jannice; and you kept the faith: Hail and farewell, sweetheart; for ever and for ever, hail and farewell!"

Rosie Redmond, on the other hand, is little more than a workaday whore, complaining about the dearth of business, trying to cadge free drinks from the bartender, hoping that every man who enters the pub will respond to her solicitations, but accepting her lot with good cheer and equanimity. Angela's professional status, however, is a bit more ambiguous: she has obviously allowed John Jo Mulligan to lure her into his apartment and seduce her, although it is soon apparent that his efforts are akin to a mouse catching a cat by sitting on its tongue. It is now the small hours of the morning, and the timid John Jo is feverishly intent on getting Angela out of his flat lest his proper landlady wake up and find her there. His Christian conscience is troubling him, but it is primarily fear of discovery that is driving him frantic. Angela, of course, has neither regrets nor apprehensions. She is happy-go-lucky and vivacious, and fully aware of what a measly mouse her escort actually is. To exasperate him she pretends to look for her lipstick, accuses him of taking advantage of a defenseless girl, insists that she came in with a purse that she now cannot find, and feigns a swooning spell—all of which drives Mulligan to distraction. Taking full advantage of his cowardly fear of the landlady, Angela manages to exact magnificent reparations for the loss of her innocence, and through one ruse or another (as well as through his fear-provoked carelessness) she manages to saunter out with Mulligan's coat and umbrella, wearing his expensive ring, and carrying off his wallet and money, including a check that he had written to buy her off. O'Casey comments that Angela Nightingale is "far and away too good a companion of an hour, a year, or a life, for a fellow like Mulligan," and he allows the delightful Angela to ride roughshod over the terrified prude.

O'Casey's young heroines share with the mother-figures of his plays a unique position: they far out-number the male heroes, most of his men being too weak and too conventional to rival the strong-minded and vibrant women. The older women, like Juno Boyle, were obviously modeled after his own mother, for whom Sean O'Casey maintained an unusually strong degree of veneration. In the autobiographies he immortalized her as Mrs. Susan Casside, and in *Red Roses* he added another portrait in Mrs. Breydon. The dual canvas gives the writer two chances at painting the portrait, but it also offers complementary techniques from which to choose. Spread over four volumes of autobiography, the view of Mrs. Casside weaves in and out of Johnny's story for forty years, and the instances of her life accumulate slowly for periodic evaluation. With her death O'Casey is profuse in his eulogy, lauding the saintly mother whose persistent love for him had protected a child thrown precariously into a hostile environment, whose understanding had been a consistent source of strength to him, and whose warmth and love of beauty

gave him the necessary insight to become an artist.
Forgotten in the final eulogies are the moments of ex-
asperation that she betrayed, the meek acquiescence to
the will of the clergy that too often brought Johnny
back to school despite the pains in his eyes, and the
failure of the mother with all of her other children
except the preferred Johnny. Yet these elements are
there in the first three volumes and presented by
O'Casey as they occur, so that a composite portrait
accumulates of a much-harried tenement mother, fighting poverty and ignorance, but herself prey to the
superstitions of her environment, and hoping that a
good word from the minister will assure her child's
future. Her moments of rebelliousness are magnificent:
when Johnny comes home drenched from Sunday
School, her usual obeisance to Reverend Hunter is
momentarily forgotten as she fulminates against the
Church: "A church that 'ud send a delicate half-starved
child home to his mother in your state is round a
corner 'n well outa the sight o' God. . . . if oul' Hunter
comes here before I forget the wettin' you got, I'll
give him a piece of me mind about the thrue 'n ever-
lastin' gospel of man mind thyself, for if you don't
no-one else will." Although this instance passes without
her opportunity to enlighten the Protestant minister,
a second one soon occurs when Johnny reacts in kind
to corporal punishment by breaking an ebony ruler
over the teacher's bald pate: "The harsh hand that
fell on him today shall not fall on him tomorrow, or
the next day, and its dark shadow shall he never see
again," she says to Hunter; "Tell that to Slogan from
the boy's mother."

The depiction of Mrs. Breydon in the play is hardly as episodic, compressed as it is into a drama of several days' endurance in which the son is essentially the main character. As he had done with Juno Boyle (presenting those facets of her character early in the play which show her to be a nagging wife and rather conservative in her apolitical stances), O'Casey introduces the dual aspects of Mrs. Breydon in the first act. She carries with her an innate superiority as a Protestant among her Catholic neighbors, but spends much of her time ministering to the sick of the neighborhood, at the reckless expense of her own health. She displays little understanding of Ayamonn's interests in the arts and little sympathy with the impending strike, and her dissection of Sheila (although accurate) is certainly unkind. And it is not just that she is perceptive about Sheila where Ayamonn is naive: her path to perception begins at her prejudice—"She's a Roman Catholic; steeped in it, too, the way she'd never forgive a one for venturin' to test the Pope's pronouncement." Her advocacy of the status quo reinforces the rather stolid attitude expressed in her resentment of Ayamonn's Catholic girl: "The bigger half of Ireland would say that a man's way with a maid must be regulated by his faith an' hers, an' the other half by the way her father makes his livin'." Yet Mrs. Breydon becomes the barometer by which audience reaction shifts decisively toward the efficacy of Ayamonn's revolutionary unionism. By Act Two she is saving the atheist Mullcanny from the outraged violence of the neighborhood, although she herself abhors his atheism, and her denunciation of Sheila's diatribe against him is most precise: "Shame on you,

Sheila, for such a smoky flame to come from such a golden lamp!" Once Ayamonn has committed himself to leading the strike, Mrs. Breydon shakes off her parochial reticence and offers her blessing to her son in his venture. She would have preferred that Reverend Clinton dissuade him from risking his life, and urges Ayamonn to stay "where safety is a green tree with a kindly growth," but finally she concedes: "Go on your way, my son, an' win. We'll welcome another inch of the world's welfare." Other mothers in O'Casey's plays prove to be ineffectual (Mrs. Heegan in *The Silver Tassie* and Jack's mother in *The Star Turns Red*) and some even selfishly vicious (Jannice's mother in *Within the Gates*), but with his creation of Mrs. Casside, Mrs. Breydon, and Juno Boyle, O'Casey achieved three of his finest portrayals.

3

The O'Casey Touch

It is a commonplace assumption that the self-taught
playwright underwent several distinct stages. His least
friendly critics would classify these as first, that period
of hit-and-miss dramaturgy which remained very close
to traditional lines but somehow accidentally produced
those early masterpieces; second, the attainment of an
overenthusiastic bravado which allowed him to experiment with expressionistic techniques rather imita-
tively and clumsily; third, the time of his most naive
immersion in ideology which produced dull and wooden
propaganda plays; and, fourth, a "sunset" stage in
which he lost complete touch with the basic Irish
sources for his material, but retained or regained his
Irish sense of the wildly comic, adding an element of
fantasy at times gay and at times obtrusive. No single
critic actually rates O'Casey exactly in this way, but
this is a composite of the general aspects of disapproval
and the most frequent touches of begrudging praise.
The common denominator of all denigration of

O'Casey's technique as a dramatist is the assumption that he never actually refined a fully conscious skill in *controlling* the important elements of his craft: that although he often created excellent pieces of drama and sketched some fine characterizations, O'Casey was never a play*wright*. Even those who insist upon O'Casey's "genius" use that term of exaggerated approbation to offset an insistence on his frequent gaffes. Yet these advocates perform an unnecessary disservice: Sean O'Casey is at his best precisely in what he had *wrought*.

Stagecraft at its most basic involves the necessity of setting a scene, and it is with this essential (often passed on instead to a designer) that O'Casey demonstrates his individual touch. The early naturalistic plays provided no difficulty for him; he was well versed in describing the basics of a tenement room, and if "photographic realism" means anything in regard to these plays, it is in such specific renderings as: "Between the window and the dresser is a picture of the Virgin; below the picture, on a bracket, is a crimson bowl in which a floating votive light is burning. Farther to the right is a small bed partly concealed by cretonne hangings strung on a twine." O'Casey would have been a poor choice indeed for an Abbey production had he not been able to pinpoint that facet of his known world, but it is in his later non-naturalistic works that his powers of evocative description are significant.

The war scene for *The Tassie* was O'Casey's first significant departure from appearances of realism. Expressionism as a movement in the theatre involved the dramatist as poetic evoker of mood through the original manipulations of the physical aspects of the stage, and O'Casey undertook the challenge with determination. Georg Kaiser and Ernst Toller, the Čapeks, Elmer Rice and Eugene O'Neill had already committed their stage to. expressionistic experiment, but O'Casey had little practical familiarity with the technique, although he attempted to learn as quickly as possible, particularly from Toller and O'Neill. The original Augustus John sets for the London production have often been praised (and recently the sets by John Bury for the Royal Shakespeare Company have been lauded as well), yet it is in O'Casey's printed demands that the excellence of the mood-setting exists. From the lengthy description can be extracted basic elements: the "jagged and lacerated ruin of what was once a monastery," "a lost wall and window . . . indicated by an arched piece of broken coping," "heaps of rubbish mark where houses once stood," "lean, dead hands . . . protruding," "spiky stumps of trees," "in the red glare . . . the criss-cross pattern of the barbed wire," "sometimes a green star, sometimes a white star," "a stained-glass window, background green, figure of the Virgin, white-faced, wearing a black robe, lights inside making the figure vividly apparent," "a life-size crucifix," "an arm from the cross . . . outstretched towards the figure of the Virgin." In addition, there is Barney tied to the gunwheel, the intrusion of "the shape of a big howitzer gun, squat, heavy underpart, with a long, sinister barrel now pointing towards the front at an angle of forty-five degrees," signs reading PRINCEPS PACIS, HYDE PARK CORNER, and

NO HAWKERS OR STREET CRIES PERMITTED HERE, the bra-
zier burning in the center of the stage, and the ghastly
figure of the Croucher on the ramp. It seems inconceiv-
able now that a director who wanted poetry in his
theatre could ever have turned a blind eye on O'Casey's
set and haggled about the playwright never having actually been to the front lines himself.

The next experiment for O'Casey was to give his
setting the physical power of internal change: instead
of creating four different areas for the action of each
of the four acts (as he had arranged in *The Plough* and
The Tassie), he returned to the single arena for the
entire development (as in *The Gunman* and *Juno*).
Gaudy new pieces of furniture added for the opening
of Act Two of *Juno* demonstrated to the audience the
effect of the legacy; the stage stripped bare when the
curtain rises again in the middle of Act Three enacts
the collapse of the windfall—but these are still the
necessary requisites of naturalistic plot changes. In
Within the Gates the park scene remains essentially the
same through all four scenes, except as the four changes
of season have naturally affected the landscape and the
shifts from morning to evening in four stages altered
the lighting. Time exists here on two levels simultaneously: most of a year has passed and yet only a
single day has been unfolded; the events of the action
have progressed at normal calendar-clock time and yet
have been compressed into an accelerated crescendo.
The barometer of emotional impact, a constant set
against the variables of time and season, is the War
Memorial, which should logically be able to withstand

these naturalistic changes. In Scene One it is described: "a War Memorial in the form of a steel-helmeted soldier, the head bent on the breast, skeleton-like hands leaning on the butt-end of a rifle"; in Scene Two the summer noon sun exacts a small measure of alteration: "The Memorial, touched by the sun, now resembles a giant clad in gleaming steel"; in Scene Three light-changes create even greater effects in mood: "The figure of the Soldier now shows a deep black against the crimson hue of the sky"; and in Scene Four it takes on the final somber note of the resolution of the dramatic conflict: "Light from an electric lamp behind the War Memorial shines on the head and shoulders of the figure, making them glow like burnished aluminium, and the bent head appears to be looking down at the life going on below it." Not only was O'Casey a poet of the theatre who made impossibly poetic demands upon the stage designer, but his eye for detail insisted that even a fixed statue undertake the movements of an accomplished actor. His next task was to make the walls of the box stage come alive and perform their artistic function.

The first indication of this accomplishment can be seen in *The Star Turns Red*, where O'Casey's ideas in color symbolism begin to affect the physical contours of the tenement scene. The room is essentially the same Dublin flat that had been the locus of the naturalistic dramas, but the walls are painted "vivid black, contrasting with the dark blue of the sky outside, seen through the windows," and the table is "covered with a yellow cloth bordered with white—the papal colours."

A picture of a bishop on the wall is balanced by one of Lenin; symbolic function overlays stage realism for the playwright of contrasting moods and genres. The black-walled tenement is followed by the scene in the green-walled Union hall and the purple-and-gold walls of the Lord Mayor's mansion, so that in each instance the eye perceives representative significance even before stage action and dialogue develop plot and characterization. Yet the technique in *The Star* only requires static symbolism, duplicated in *Behind the Green Curtains*, where the opening and closing of the curtains serve to underscore freedom from parochial restriction and the petrification of those who lack the courage to let the outside world break through. In *Purple Dust*, however, the walls begin to move. On the surface level actual refurbishing is taking place: the Englishmen are transforming a Tudor-Elizabethan mansion closer to their hearts' desire, intending to restore the beauty of the past by imposing their wretched modern taste upon a crumbling relic. O'Casey's descriptions are full of editorial comment: the room is "gloomy" and looks "like a gigantic cage," and the beams have been recently painted "to draw attention to their beauty; but the paint makes them too conspicuous and, therefore, ugly." Toward the end of the first act "plaster falls and a hole appears in the ceiling," as an overhead light fixture is being installed—in the wrong place. "Oh, they're knocking down more than they're building up!", Poges complains, with more truth than he yet realizes. In the second act Poges manipulates a gigantic lawn roller that goes out of control; "a rumbling crash of falling

bricks and mortar" is heard, and the news is brought
back that he "has gone right through the wall with the
the roller, an' shook the house—bang!" But these are
minor harbingers of the cataclysm to come: the final
moments of *Purple Dust* depict the coming of the Flood
—"the green waters tumble into the room through the
entrance from the hall," as visual reality demonstrates
symbolic change.

The same kind of change is operative in *Oak Leaves
and Lavender*, but now under conditions of total transformation. O'Casey begins with one of the most
traditional of stage settings (quite uncharacteristic of
his own milieu) : "The great room of a Manorial House
of a long-past century, when the lights are low, and the
flickering shadows softly come and go." In contrast to
his expressed prejudice against the purple-dust decay
of the previous mansion, he presents this one in all its
preserved glory as a masterpiece of architectural beauty
—his intentions here are not anarchistic (bring the past
tumbling down so that the future can build on its ruins)
but communistic (take over and transform into utility
the best structures that have thus far been preserved) .
In his stage directions he hypothesizes a "dreamy en-
gineer" who might look with imaginative eyes on the
sculptured beauty of the room and envision its next
stage of development. Such a planner, O'Casey speculates, might see "the rods and motionless shafts of
machinery" in the chiseled panelling, "revolving cog-
wheels" in the back walls, "gigantic gantries" in the
chandeliers, and so forth. Nothing has yet actually
changed: the romantic past still has its consistent hold

on the rococco splendor of the ancient room as the
ghostly dancers dominate it in the Prelude. By the
beginning of Act One, a slight indication is offered
that "the panelling seems a little stylised away from
its normal lines and curving." The spirit of change is
personified in a "sturdy young foreman" who "speaks
with an Irish accent," a somewhat mysterious figure
who appears in the third act to tell of the death of Edgar
and Jennie, but stays on for a while to order Feelim
about and praise de Valera; he reappears toward the
end of the act to announce, briskly: "Now, ladies and
gentlemen, murmur your last farewell, and take your
last look at the house of your fathers; for in a few
minutes' time we link this with the other factory turning
out tanks for the Red Army, and tanks for our own."
The opening of the act already contains the blueprint
for change:

> The scene is the same, but the aspect of the big room has
> changed with the changing world outside it. Its broad
> and pleasing panelling has become like the ties, the belts,
> and bars connecting various parts of machinery together,
> and making of them an active, unified whole. The capa-
> cious fireplace, resembling it before, has now assumed
> the almost similar—though something stylised—shape of
> a great drop-hammer. The columns flanking the doorway
> have become machinery shafts.

This descriptive passage is a lengthy and detailed one,
but it still presents only a stationary façade, an immobile
backdrop to the human action of the play. Once the
Foreman blows his whistle, however,

> the room becomes alive with movement—the belts travel,
> the wheels turn, and the drop-hammer rises and falls.

The central wheel is yellow as the ripening corn; the smaller ones red as the setting sun; and the travelling-belts green as dewy grass on a fine spring morning. Through the window, the silhouette of the great crane's jib is seen, holding in its beak the silhouette of a tank that is swung by the window, down to the ground. The modified clank of steel touching steel is heard, accompanied by the sounds indicating the busy and orderly hustle of a factory.

With this technique O'Casey has created a symbolic setting, brought it to life and had it undergo vital changes, while counterpointing the plot of the drama and making a political statement in its own eloquent voice. Here in *Oak Leaves* the device is employed for its greatest potential, although the playwright used it in other ways thereafter: in *Cock-a-Doodle Dandy* the Marthraun house shakes and shivers during the exorcism, and the flagpole flying the Irish tricolor comes tumbling down.

O'Casey's attention to color symbolism is occasional rather than consistent, although certain definite patterns exist within the canon of his work. The purple of the Tudor dust, for example, is probably literal and poetic, not necessarily emblematic. Yet the possibility of a royal purple being washed away by green floodwaters carries definite weight. (Purple and gold in the Lord Mayor's house is exact representation of official pomp, a representation that is significantly different from the suggestiveness of symbolism; the papal table cloth again is direct commentary.) For Mrs. Casside and Mrs. Breydon the author chooses a trinity of flowers, geraniums, fuchsia, and musk, the three colors of red, gold, and purple thereafter taking on a representative

function for the flowers which symbolize the most positive essence of these mother figures. In the ugliness of
tenement life these women shelter their fragile blooms
in biscuit tins under the window: Mrs. Breydon fears
for them when rocks are thrown into the room in an
attack on the atheistic Mullcanny, while Mrs. Casside
is concerned about the welfare of her flowers when she
is ill and Johnny neglects them. O'Casey describes them
in *Red Roses*: "These crimson, gold, and purple flowers
give a regal tint to the poor room"; in *Drums under the
Window* he circumscribes the small world of his
mother: "She would get her last look at a patch of sky
through the crooked window, over the tops of the musk,
the geraniums, and the fuchsia—that would be her way
to a further life." Both of these works were written
immediately after the Spanish Civil War, and the tricolor of the Republican flag may have suggested the
arrangement to the dramatist. In the earlier *I Knock at
the Door* the exact symmetry does not yet exist, the
flowers presented merely as "two geraniums, one white,
the other red, and the purple-cloaked fuchsia"; this
may have been literal reality, while the emblematic
colors suggested themselves later as political symbolism.
With the mother's death Sean Casside abandons the
room *they* had lived in and the flowers that his mother
had loved, breaking off sprigs of each to place in her
dead hand under the shroud, and covering her coffin
with a red flag. (This symbolic nuance carries over into
Oak Leaves, where Monica wraps a strip of green cloth
over the British flag that drapes Drishogue's coffin.)
The trinity of flowers is perpetuated even further in the

autobiographies, becoming symbolic of the writer's career. He translates his mother's touch of beauty into his own concern with artistic beauty, at first beginning to "set down sad thoughts in bad verses, which was his little space of geranium, fuchsia, and musk," until bad verses are replaced by good prose: "halo'd by whirling crimson gerontium disks, and encompassed about with the blowing of mosque-scented trumpets of gold, and the pealing of purple con fuchsian bells." The artistic inspiration which came from his mother's flowers engenders the poetic symbolism of his craft as a literary artist.

O'Casey attached almost magical properties to an occasional touch of color which, like his mother's flowers, breaks the gloom of drab reality or rescues those who are potentially alive from the death-grip of their environment. Mary Boyle is at her best when she debates between a green ribbon or a blue one for her hair when dressing to go out on the picket line, while Minnie Powell's brown costume is "crowned by a silk tam-o'-shanter of a rich blue tint." In *The Plough*, however, the playwright is careful to avoid the use of bright colors for the dress of either Nora Clitheroe or Rosie Redmond, since the former is clothed to represent her bourgeois pretensions (a silver fox fur) and the latter her profession (a low-cut blouse). Nor is Jessie Taite in *The Tassie* in any way redeemed by a splash of color, her party dress being significant only because of its sexual suggestiveness: "Jessie has on a very pretty, rather tight-fitting dance frock, with the sleeves falling widely to the elbow, and cut fairly low on her breast."

It is with Jannice in *The Gates* that the vivid splash of
color begins to become a dominant motif, as expressionistic design takes over from literal verisimilitude; her
black costume is offset by a scarlet hat, and the black
crescent in the hat is balanced by the scarlet crescent
on the hip of her dress. These two areas of color for
the clothing of the young woman thereafter become
patterns, the blue-green subdued but definite indication
of the Life Force, and the brightly vivid reds and
oranges that burst forth as dominant symbols of that
Force. In *Red Roses*, for example, Sheila Moorneen,
whose redemption is always in doubt until the closing
minutes of the play, is described by the author only
upon her first entrance (after Ayamonn has exalted
her and his mother cut her down to size) , and the blue
touch is the only indication that she might at some time
be the ideal beloved of bare feet and black shawl and
red roses that Ayamonn has envisioned: her tailored
suit of brown is quite standard, and her "golden-brown
blouse" traditional enough, but her hat is significantly
"bright-blue." This piece of slightly-symbolic verisimilitude is later enlivened in the fantasy scene of Act Three,
where the despondently drab Finnoola unfolds into a
distinct but quiet magnificence: she "is dressed in a
skirt of brighter green than the other two women, a
white bodice slashed with black, and a flowing silvery
scarf is round her waist." At the other end of the spectrum is Angela Nightingale, who comes out of the bed-
room in characteristic disarray: "She has put on her
stockings—silk ones—and skirt, a short, well-tailored one
of darkish green, with broad belt of dark red and black

buckle. She carries a brown jersey over her arm, and her shoes in her hand."

The other O'Caseyan heroines are thus easily recognizable by either their strong touch of picturesque rebellion and defiance or by the quieter nuance. Scarlet is of course the mode of the temptress, from Jannice's crescent to Angela's red belt; in *Cock-a-Doodle Dandy* it surfaces in its full glory, Loreleen wearing "a darkish green dress, with dark-red flashes on bodice and side of skirt." To this O'Casey adds "a saucy hat of a brighter green" that "sports a scarlet ornament, its shape suggestive of a cock's crimson crest." (Even the male Messenger of *Cock* has a "pair of scarlet wings" emblazoned on his coat, and wears green sandals and beret.) When the scarlet ornament on Loreleen's hat comes to life and frightens the old men with its symbolic depiction of the "evil" they fear, it is the Life Force manifesting itself in the saucy personalities of young and beautiful women. With Monica Penrhyn both aspects of the suggestion of color are presented: her nightclothes in the second act are trimmed in blue, while in her first appearance she is wearing the usual brown with a "gaily-coloured scarf" over her hair, a scarf that does multiple service in the later plays. The Widda Machree in "Time to Go" confronts the same sort of mercantile-minded stalwarts as the three heroines do in *Cock-a-Doodle Dandy*: she has come to a fair in a small Irish town to sell her cow, and having sold it to Kelly from the Isle of Mananaun, she feels guilty for having exacted too high a price. Her concern is matched by Kelly himself, who feels he has been allowed to pay less for it than

he should have. This revolutionary standard of business
ethics brings the two together, but it outrages the local
merchants and farmers who have long since committed
themselves totally to the profit motive, and even the
small farmer drained dry by the power of the larger
owners and businessmen tacitly accepts the system. Kelly
and the Widda undergo a miraculous transformation
with which the locals are incapable of coping, and, in
an attempt to preserve the status quo, they call in the
constabulary. But the two rebels have also undergone
transformations into the miraculous, attaining supernatural powers (like the Cock) to fly by their nets. It
is not surprising, therefore, to recall that the lovely
Widda wears a colored scarf and a bright blue cloak.
(Nora McGilligan wears a blue skirt, and she and the
other girls of *The Drums* have "brightly-coloured ker-
chiefs round their necks, or worn peasant-wise round
their heads"; Reena Kilternan's dress is described as
"a little austere and sober"—she is of course a devoutly
compliant Catholic—"but a gay-coloured scarf around
her neck pays a tribute to youth and loveliness.")

When Keelin Reiligan hints that her frigid sister
Foorawn (her name in Irish denotes just that) actually
hides beneath her blue-black somber clothing an element of soft stuff of silk and nylon, she is intimating
that Foorawn's rejection of Manus exists only on the
surface, that she harbors a repressed love for him. The
intimation is corroborated only at the end of the drama,
when she confesses her love for the man who has killed
her. Silk and nylon hose in particular are also O'Caseyan
barometers of vital feminine characteristics: Keelin's

nylons are amber; Angela's are silk; both Reena and Bernadette Shillayley wear nylons, the latter's are a "first-class pair"; Loreleen's legs come in for even greater attention, since they are "very charming ones" and "clad in brown silk stockings; brown that flashes a golden sheen"; and maid Marion also has "nice legs, and she likes to show them—and why shouldn't she?" Particularly in *Cock-a-Doodle Dandy*, but also in most of the later plays, O'Casey pays special attention to feminine allure, even to the extent of condoning the practice of sexual teasing of prudish and sex-frightened males. Angela Nightingale's demolition of the timid John Jo Mulligan is only one of several examples. Keelin taunts the mousy Rankin by displaying her nyloned legs, and he reacts violently by spitting in her face; in *The Star* flirtatious Julia tries to get the terrified Joybell to kiss her, but he responds by lustfully attacking her; the situation is reversed in *Green Curtains* when Christy Kornavaun, the Catholic journalist who disapproves of Noneen working in Chatastray's house, tries to embrace her and gets a drink thrown into his face; while in *The Drums of Father Ned* Bernadette duplicates Angela's triumph, pretending that the Ulster businessman Skerighan has so flustered her with his attentions that she is near fainting, exacting several pounds from the worried man before running off in delight. From *The Gunman* on O'Casey equated the pretty girl in pretty clothes with a vibrant love of life, in significant contrast to the mean existences of sex-fearing males. The Jack O'Killigains are rare in their ability to respond in kind and degree to the lively sexuality of the young heroines. Donal the poltroon (and to a greater extent John Jo Mulligan) represents the typical male in the world depicted by Sean O'Casey, where young women seem to hold life securely in their warm hands. "Well, you take care not to hurt yourself when you're kind to a girl," Daisy Battles says when Sean Casside steals a kiss, and she soon relieves him of his torn trousers, dropping her own green shawl, "leaving her in chemise and stockings." When Casside prepares to leave for work several hours later, Daisy comments, "you've learned a lot with me today, haven't you? You'll be a knowin' fellow from this out."

A pretty face, an ample bosom, and tantalizing legs may seem more appropriate for Hollywood than for serious drama, but O'Casey sees them as hopeful signs of life worth living. In addition he resorts to non-descriptive editorial comments on these young women, suggesting a pattern of thought that pervades the plays. Mary Boyle's split between the conditions of life that threaten to submerge her and the literature she had read that might pull her through presents an early indication of such editorialization. (The proof of the author's suppositions are always in the context of the play itself, however.) With Minnie Powell it is not literature, but a degree of self-assurance that from the outset delineates her character and determines her course of action: "The fact of being forced to earn her living, and to take care of herself, on account of her parents' early death, has given her an assurance beyond her years. She has lost the sense of fear (she does not know this), and, consequently, she is at ease in all places and before all persons, even those of a superior

education, so long as she meets them in an atmosphere
that surrounds the members of her own class." This
sort of lengthy commentary probably derived from
O'Casey's reading of Bernard Shaw's stage descriptions,
usurping the novelist's function but also setting the
standards for subsequent characterization at a high
level of attainment. It is "easy confidence" that Minnie
has to prove to an audience, and her handling of the
Mills bombs is adequate substantiation. In contrast to
Minnie is poor Nora Clitheroe, who fails where Minnie
succeeds—in standing up to "the circumstances of her
life." O'Casey's initial description of Nora postulates
the equivocal condition of her personality: although
he allows that she is "alert, swift, full of nervous en-
ergy," he also indicates that she is "a little anxious to
get on in the world." The opposing forces at work on
the young housewife are then codified: "The firm
lines of her face are considerably opposed by a soft,
amorous mouth and gentle eyes. When her firmness
fails her, she persuades with her feminine charm." The
editorialization here is oblique; firmness of character
and the use of female allure are both advantageous, but
Nora's concern with getting on in the world is the particular danger. Misguided motivation becomes her
major problem, and neither her femininity nor her
strength will be able to redirect her. Her desire to
"get on" is only a venial sin; the destruction of all her
hopes at the end of *The Plough* is an excessive punishment for so frail a creature with such harmless desires.

In *The Silver Tassie* O'Casey doubled his concern
in creating both Susie Monican and Jessie Taite. Neither was destined for the tragic eventualities that

awaited Minnie and Nora, but each was in herself an interesting manifestation of O'Casey's interest in the character of the young woman. With Jessie the totality is already present in the author's initial evaluation:

> Jessie is twenty-two or so, responsive to all the animal impulses of life. Ever dancing around, in and between the world, the flesh, and the devil. She would be happy climbing with a boy among the heather on Howth Hill, and could play ball with young men on the swards of Phoenix Park. She gives her favour to the prominent and popular. Harry is her favourite: his strength and speed has won the Final for his club, he wears the ribbon of the D.C.M. It is a time of spiritual and animal exultation for her.

There is an undoubtedly significant note of admiration for her exuberant vitality in this descriptive passage, but there is no doubt either that Jessie is incapable of loyalty to a defeated hero. Her defection to the new favorite, Barney Bagnal, elicits no surprise: her few lines in Act One are enough to corroborate the suspicion that Jessie's concerns are egocentric and shallow: "You'll not forget to send me the German helmet home from France, Harry?" On the other hand, Susie's change is expected to be astonishing, from religious fanatic to vivacious enchantress; yet the author has been careful to prepare the ground for the change. He describes her as "a girl of twenty-two, well-shaped limbs, challenging breasts" (the physical equipment necessary to seduce Dr. Maxwell) , but "all of which are defiantly hidden by a rather long dark blue skirt and bodice buttoning up to the throat"—a costume as forbidding as Foorawn's. His description is soon repeated: "She is undeniably pretty, but her charms are almost completely hidden by her sombre, ill-fitting dress, and the rigid manner in which she has made her hair up declares her unflinching and uncompromising modesty." The alert spectator, however, should immediately be suspicious of her "crimson scarf," and not too surprised when her repressed sexuality is lavished on Harry Heegan, so that even Jessie is jealous enough of her attentions to pull Harry away from her. The crimson touch of color is again an immediate emblem.

Jannice, the Young Whore of *The Gates*, is awarded an almost complete measure of O'Casey's devotion. There is no aspect of her pathetic death and frightened life that derives intrinsically from her own personality. Jannice has mustered whatever strength she is capable of in order to withstand constant misfortune, and she dies valiantly. The author's own statements on her character are as close to being unequivocal as he ever gets; after praising her physical beauty, and bemoaning the pallor that already hints at her imminent death, he makes his basic statements:

> She has an intelligent look, which is becoming a little worn by contact with the selfishness and meanness of the few clients that have patronised her; for these, though unable to resist the desire to have her, hate her subconsciously before they go with her, and consciously detest her when their desires have been satisfied. She has read a little, but not enough; she has thought a little, but not enough; she is deficient in self-assurance, and is too generous and sensitive to be a clever whore, and her heart is not in the business.

A recourse to literature is offered as a partial solution to Jannice's situation—as it had been for Mary Boyle—

but proves too limited, as it had for O'Casey's sister Isabella. A need for self-confidence (Minnie's fortunate achievement through the accident of orphanage) is stressed as paramount, but as we learn from the Atheist's biographical details, the absence of parents has tended to deny Jannice self-assurance rather than establish it. These two bodies of information, the O'Caseyan stage direction and the Atheist's comments, reinforce the background conditions that affect Jannice: she is in constant combat with the fears instilled by religion despite her insistence on making her own way in the world. O'Casey is at his most purposeful ambiguity when he depicts her making a sign of the cross before dying, but having its resultant effect on the Dreamer remain negligible. To the extent that Jannice can control her own life, she is magnificent, but in those areas absolutely beyond her powers she is pathetically fragile.

The deficiencies of those young heroines whom O'Casey created and presented but could breathe little life into are immediately discernible from his paucity of description. Julia of *The Star* is acknowledged to be "pretty" and "vigorous," but he has nothing else to say about her. Monica Penrhyn, for all her courageous defiance in marrying Drishogue and insisting on conceiving a child that will assure her husband's perpetuation, receives little more notice from O'Casey, except for her beauty: that her eyes are "a little pensive at times" is important, as is the statement that she is "a girl who would be able to concentrate on what was actually before her to do." There is no prevailing complexity here, no conflict between external forces and internal strengths and weaknesses, and consequently a rather straight line of development in her character and her situation. Her friend Jennie, on the other hand, receives a closer degree of scrutiny:

> Jennie is a sturdy lass, inclined to be slightly florid, and though she is fairly well educated as things go, having had a secondary schooling, she is at times somewhat rough and strident in her manner. She is enticingly shaped, even a little voluptuous-looking. She has a head of thick, dark, honey-yellow hair which she often tosses aside when she feels it clustering on her forehead. She is twenty-four, full of confidence, and likes to be thought a little Rabelaisian.

This is a wealth of commentary to lavish on a secondary character (and O'Casey is careful to keep Jennie relatively minor compared to Monica, as Edgar is kept minor in comparison with Drishogue), but it is also expended in contrast to another Land Girl, the Joy who is in every way only a pale reflection of Jennie. The playwright's purpose eventually becomes apparent: Jennie harbors the capacity of unusual heroism, an act of sacrifice which will startle everyone. Although her lover Edgar is lukewarm in his love for her (admitting to Drishouge that it does not go beyond the delights of the nighttime), Jennie is wholeheartedly committed to him, and her death in his arms amid the burning ruin of his plane is amazingly heroic no matter which version one believes: that she attempted against incredible odds to drag him from the wreckage or that she insisted on dying with him. Just as the imperfect Feelim is a far more successful rendering of character than the too-perfect Drishogue, so Jennie has a more individual spark in her than the perfectly balanced Monica.

Far more successful as the Rabelaisian female whose lust for life results in perpetuation and augmentation of life is the delightful Avril of *Purple Dust*. She has made the best of a bad situation by attaching herself to a wealthy Englishman and agreeing to take up residence in the ancient Tudor mansion, but maintains her own independence throughout. Her flirtation with O'Killigain may have remained only that but for his playful "sharp skelp on the behind," forcing her to either insist on her privileged position as mistress of the house or abandon the pretense and accept Jack as her lover. From that point Avril moves defiantly in her own direction, progressively abandoning Basil Stoke for the manly O'Killigain. Nonetheless, O'Casey's introduction to her contains many qualifiers:

> She is a pretty girl of twenty-one or so, inclined, at times, to be a little romantic, and is very much aware of her good looks. She is far from being unintelligent, but she does little and cares less about developing her natural talents. Her eyes are large and expressive, but sometimes sink into a hardened lustre. She is inclined to think that every good-looking young fellow, rich or poor, should fall for her pretty face and figure, and is a little worried if one of them doesn't.

There is enough in this critique to suggest a shallowness that equals the flaws which contribute to Nora Clitheroe's destruction, but *Purple Dust* is merely intended as a "wayward comedy," so that any larger development of the possibilities of Avril's complex personality would have been excessive within the context. It is apparent from his description, however, that O'Casey saw many facets to the potentiality of characters like Avril and had to allow himself to be confined by the genre.

Where there is room and opportunity for a young heroine to develop, O'Casey avails himself of it, as in *Red Roses for Me*. Here the conflicting views of Ayamonn and his mother introduce the young woman long before she appears, and it is apparent that she will have to demonstrate the real aspects of herself in contradistinction to one or both of the versions presented. When she does appear, she is described by O'Casey in terms of her physical grace and beauty, with an emphasis on her "sympathetic" eyes, which "dim, now and again, with a cloud of timidity." The positive quality of sympathy is contrasted with an implied lack of self-assurance; this is reinforced by lovely hair which is tied in a thick bun, and brown clothes offset by a "bright-blue hat." Finally, there is her immediate manner: "She comes in shyly, evidently conscious of Mrs. Breydon's presence, but fighting her timidity with a breezy and jovial demeanour." The symptoms are now apparent: if Sheila can overcome her reticence and assert the strength that lies beneath the surface (if the long hair can break loose from its confining coil), she will move closer to the idealization held by Ayamonn and away from Mrs. Breydon's suspicions of her. The single piece of positive evidence comes early in the last act, when Sheila accompanies Mrs. Breydon to St. Burnupus' church, both intent on dissuading Ayamonn from endangering his life. Although she also attempts to dissuade the Police Inspector from attacking the strikers, Sheila does not yet reach the level attained by Ayamonn's mother, who finally blesses her son's endeavor, but she does allow herself to be persuaded by Reverend Clinton to enter the Protestant church for a cup of tea. The death of Ayamonn effects the transition totally: she denounces the Inspector and declares herself a partisan of her dead lover and his living ideals, justifying the full significance of her "large, sympathetic brown eyes."

Later heroines like Monica are relatively uncomplicated and unifaceted, especially the three women in *Cock-a-Doodle Dandy*: Loreleen has a "jaunty air" that is "the sign of a handsome, gay, and intelligent woman," and is attractively dressed as well; Marion of the lovely legs adds to the loveliness of her limbs "the spice of a saucy look to her bright blue eyes"; and Lorna, almost an afterthought as a character, is "good-looking still," with "bright and graceful contours" to her face. Yet for Lorna is added a condition: her face shows that she is "somewhat troubled by a vague aspect of worry and inward timidity." Being slightly older than the other two girls, she shares Souhaun's concern that her opportunities for escape may not be so definite. Yet when the climax of the ugly situation in Nyadnanave occurs, and Loreleen is driven from the town, it is Lorna who makes the conscious and valiant decision to accompany her, with Marion trailing after. The resolution of her troubled countenance comes with her voluntary action. Lorna is most like Reena Kilternan, about whom O'Casey says very little by way of introduction, except in indicating the contrast between her somber clothes

and her colored scarf, but who learns from her experience that even compliance with *most* of the strictures
of her society will not be enough, that she will have to
make a conscious break. At first she attaches herself
romantically to Dennis Chatastray, a good compromise
between conformity, inasmuch as he seems secure as
a pillar of society, and individuality, inasmuch as she
will encourage him to live idyllically away from the
center of conformity; yet he proves thoroughly cowed
by the "forces of his life," and she transfers her hopes
and affection to the Red she had previously viewed with
horror, Martin Boeman.

It is apparent that O'Casey reads the character of
his creations from telltale signs in their faces and their
eyes, that he attributes to his people characteristics
which are discernible to a practiced eye from a closer
look at facial features. This is particularly true of the
venerated mother figures. Yet his depiction of his first
successful mother-characterization gives less of a hint of
the outcome of the play from the features of the face;
of Juno Boyle he notes:

> She is forty-five years of age, and twenty years ago she
> must have been a pretty woman; but her face has now
> assumed that look which ultimately settles down upon
> the faces of the women of the working-class; a look of
> listless monotony and harassed anxiety, blending with
> an expression of mechanical resistance. Were circum-
> stances favourable, she would probably be a handsome,
> active and clever woman.

Circumstances have not been favorable, and except
for the momentary illusion of a windfall, they become

even less so. There is nothing in this description of Juno, therefore, to prepare the reader for the resilience with which she withstands ultimate adversity, when "mechanical resistance" (an essentially conservative force that makes her a nagging wife) evolves into the radical and constructive force of passionate and human resistance. Other mothers hardly fare as well, and in some cases O'Casey despairs of them from the very beginning. It is obvious that Mrs. Heegan is not going to be strong enough to be of even the most cursory aid to her wounded son. She is older than her husband, "stiffened with age and rheumatism; the end of her life is unknowingly lumbering towards a rest: the impetus necessity has given to continual toil and striving is beginning to slow down, and everything she has to do is done with a quiet mechanical persistence." It will surprise no one that "mechanical persistence" fares even worse than "mechanical resistance." (And the nameless Old Women of *Within the Gates* and *The Star Turns Red*, the mothers of Jannice and Jack, are irrevocably beyond the pale.)

A unique mother in the O'Casey collection of plays is Dame Hatherleigh who, like Monica and Feelim, remains to bear the brunt of the tragic deaths in *Oak Leaves and Lavender*. She is introduced in terms which augur all aspects of later events upon her:

She often has a brisk manner, but almost always a look of anxiety clouds her face. She is a woman of forty-five or so, well figured, though tending, ever so slightly, towards plumpness. She still holds on to a good part of an earlier loveliness shown in a heavy mass of brown hair, tinged now with grey specks; fine, oval face, and eyes, deep, dark, alert, and intelligent, perhaps a little brighter than they should be.

It is clear that O'Casey has injected a personal affection for the British woman, endowing her with aspects of his own Irish mother, but also with touches of the Anglo-Irish Lady Gregory, whom he describes in *Inishfallen* as having an "odd dignity." Dame Hatherleigh's series of shocks are as intense as Juno's (although of a very different substance), but she is in no way prepared for such sudden adversity. The war exacts its toll on all—those who have built up an endurance to suffering and those who have thus far been spared—and the bright glimmer in the Dame's eyes already suggests an incipient madness. Even before the deaths of her husband and son she is babbling absurdly about the lost tribes of Israel and digging up the Hill of Tara, and Feelim is already conditioned to humoring her. The actual deaths she can handle a great deal better than the forebodings: she is stoic in not revealing her news to anyone, but continuing on relentlessly and tirelessly with her war work. The effect upon her transforms a middle-aged woman of strength and stoicism into a broken old woman. In the third act "the Dame comes in slowly. She is covered with a long black robe; the one bright thing about her is a silver cap. Her face is mask-like in its lines of resignation. No colour, and little life is in her voice." Nonetheless, she is able to comfort Monica's father, whose farm has been destroyed and whom everyone else hates or fears. As she goes to her death, to join the dancers of the graceful past who inhabit the haunted reaches of her house, she nonetheless gives her blessing to the future, acknowledging that her house must accept the transformation into a factory. Only the beauty of the past will be preserved— all else must go. "We all must go soon," she says in her toneless voice; "Our end makes but a beginning for others."

The autobiographic Mrs. Breydon is introduced with the utmost of simplicity. Her clothes reveal only the poverty of her slum existence; she "is coming up to fifty, her face brownish, dark eyes with a fine glint in them, and she bears on her cheeks and brow the marks of struggle and hard work." Those last elements are the badges of heroism in the O'Caseyan mother, the indication of humor in the glint in her eyes and the ability to resist those forces of life which inflict toil and hardship. The balance is necessary: humorless martyrdom is offensive to O'Casey, to whom a kind of resilience to adversity coupled with a joy in life are essential, especially for the older woman with only her own strength of character to rely on. Even the aristo- cratic Lady Gregory is described in the same terms, despite the wide gulf that separates her from the all- suffering slum woman: "Her face was a rugged one," O'Casey attests in his "Blessed Bridget O'Coole" chapter of *Inishfallen,* "hardy as that of a peasant, curiously lit with an odd dignity, and softened with a careless touch of humour in the bright eyes and the curving wrinkles crowding around the corners of the firm little mouth. She looked like an old, elegant nun of a new order, a blend of the Lord Jesus Christ and of Puck, an order that Ireland had never known before, and wasn't likely to know again for a long time to come." Given the opportunity to expand his descriptive and commentative powers in the narrative prose, O'Casey arrives at the same sort of formula that his succinct stage directions indicate—that toughness and a sense of laughter combine in the older woman into a weapon against the "forces of life."

There is only his own mother then to provide the final evidence of O'Casey's reverence of a particular type of person, and the descriptive capsule which became his trademark as a dramatist. In *Inishfallen* he commends Mrs. Casside's "bravery, her irreducible and quiet endurance, her fearless and cheery battle with a hard, and often brutal, life," again coalescing the dual factors of good humor and toughness in confronting hardships. The pattern is extended further when O'Casey classifies these attributes of his mother as "the soul of Socialism," so that despite her actual political indifference he drapes her coffin in red.

During the decade in which he was carefully portraying Mrs. Casside through four volumes of autobiography, O'Casey had ample opportunity to develop, balance, intensify, and evaluate the character he was creating. Both at the beginning and toward the end he used his descriptive powers to make his individual statements, introducing Johnny's mother in *I Knock at the Door*:

> Forty years of age the woman was when the boy was three, with hair still raven black, parted particularly down the middle of the head, gathered behind in a simple coil, and kept together by a couple of hairpins; a small nose

spreading a little at the bottom; deeply set, softly gleaming brown eyes that sparkled when she laughed and hardened to a steady glow through any sorrow, deep and irremediable. . . . But it was the mouth that arrested attention most, for here was shown the chief characteristic of the woman: it quivered with fighting perseverence, firmness, human humour, and the gentle, lovable fullness of her nature. . . . A laugh that began in a ripple of humour, and ended in a musical torrent of full-toned mirth which shook those who listened into an irresistible companionship.

Many years later she again poses for her son, first for a rather terse sketch near the end of *Drums under the Window* ("She must be getting on for eighty now. She who had been buxom, was worn away now to a wiry thinness. She was a brave woman; something of the stoic in her. Seldom he had seen her cry") and later in a tribute at the beginning of *Inishfallen, Fare Thee Well*:

> Tired of singing, he had read to her from Scott and Dickens, stopping often to listen to her young, fresh, and gleaming laughter, so strange from one who had gone through so hard, bitter, and thankless a life for nearly eighty years; fifty of them little less than terrible; years that had withheld joy, raiment, food, and even hope; for she never had a hope that she could ever be better than she was. But she was always a proud woman, hating charity as an enemy, and never welcoming it, so that all these bitter years had never mastered her, never diminished the sturdiness of her fine nature.

The skill with which Sean O'Casey could capsulize into character description that handful of personality elements which encompass a person proved doubly useful throughout his career: in expanded form he was able to write the autobiography of himself and the multiple biography of the world he knew, and in concise dramatic form he etched those few strokes to delineate a character as he saw it in his mind's eye, and then allowed that character to prove himself by acting out his own personality in response to the events that confronted him. Whenever he assumed the novelist's prerogative in editorializations about his fictional people, he was careful to justify that usurpation by embodying the underlined characteristics in speech and in action, often giving his initial stage descriptions the benefit of hindsight. The play was very much the thing in which he caught conscience and character, subtleties and significance. A master of characterization for the stage O'Casey need never have been suspicious of the full validity of Lady Gregory's praise. When a political age demanded the obvious, he was unfortunately caught up in an attempt to assault his audience with the necessity of immediate commitments and the efficacy of political action; but these instances were rare. More often he was skilled in making political statements and revealing the strongest of his personal ideals through the simple expedients of setting a scene and introducing a human being onto his stage. Few committed artists in the theatre have been as successful in having reality and poetry carry the major responsibility for the writer's convictions as has Sean O'Casey.

Selected Bibliography

I. PRIMARY

Collected Plays Vol. 1 (London: Macmillan, 1949) : *Juno and the Paycock, The Shadow of a Gunman, The Plough and the Stars*, "The End of the Beginning," "A Pound on Demand."

Collected Plays Vol. 2 (London: Macmillan, 1949) : *The Silver Tassie, Within the Gates, The Star Turns Red.*

Collected Plays Vol. 3 (London: Macmillan, 1951) : *Purple Dust, Red Roses for Me*, "Hall of Healing."

Collected Plays Vol. 4 (London: Macmillan, 1951) : *Oak Leaves and Lavender, Cock-a-Doodle Dandy*, "Bedtime Story," "Time to Go."

The Bishop's Bonfire (New York: Macmillan, 1955).

The Drums of Father Ned (New York: St. Martin's Press, 1960).

Behind the Green Curtains, "Figuro in the Night," "The Moon Shines on Kylenamoe" (London: Macmillan, 1961).

I Knock at the Door (New York: Macmillan, 1939).

Pictures in the Hallway (New York: Macmillan, 1942).

Drums under the Window (New York: Macmillan, 1946).

Inishfallen, Fare Thee Well (New York: Macmillan, 1954).

Rose and Crown (New York: Macmillan, 1952).

Sunset and Evening Star (New York: Macmillan, 1954).

Mirror in My House (collection of the six autobiographies listed above) ; (New York: Macmillan, 1956).

Windfalls (London: Macmillan, 1934).

The Flying Wasp (London: Macmillan, 1937).

The Green Crow (New York: George Braziller, 1956).

Feathers from the Green Crow (ed. Robert Hogan; Columbia: University of Missouri Press, 1962).

Under a Colored Cap (New York: St. Martin's Press, 1963).

Blasts and Benedictions (ed. Ronald Ayling; New York: St. Martin's Press, 1967).

* *The Sean O'Casey Reader* (New York: St. Martin's Press, 1969).

[Various other editions, particularly of the plays, are also available.]

II. SECONDARY (BOOKS AND PAMPHLETS)

*	Armstrong, William A.	*Sean O'Casey* (London: Longmans, Green and Co., 1967).
**	Ayling, Ronald (ed.)	*Sean O'Casey* (London: Macmillan, 1969).
*	Cowasjee, Saros.	*Sean O'Casey: The Man Behind the Plays* (London: Oliver and Boyd, 1963).
*	————.	*O'Casey* (London: Oliver and Boyd, 1966).
	Fallon, Gabriel.	*Sean O'Casey: The Man I Knew* (London: Routledge and Kegan Paul, 1965).
	Hogan, Robert.	*The Experiments of Sean O'Casey* (New York: St. Martin's Press, 1960).
	Koslow, Jules.	*The Green and the Red: Sean O'Casey, the Man and His*

———

*Also contain valuable bibliographic materials.

**Contains the best and most current bibliography of secondary material on O'Casey, including items in foreign languages and in periodicals.

Krause, David. *Plays* (New York: Golden Griffin Books, 1950).

Sean O'Casey: The Man and His Work (New York: Macmillan, 1960).

———. *A Self-Portrait of the Artist as a Man: Sean O'Casey's Letters* (Dublin: Dolmen Press, 1968).

Malone, Maureen. *The Plays of Sean O'Casey* (Carbondale: Southern Illinois University Press, 1969).